Praise for *On My Honor, I Will*

———————— ✳ ————————

Randy Pennington has "cracked the code" of great leadership in *On My Honor, I Will*. He covers the broad subject of leadership without obscuring its basic elements, which are simple and long-lasting: honesty, integrity, hard work, and the golden rule. True leaders are not just bosses. True leaders are those who have mastered leadership and practice its basic principles every day. The ultimate test of leadership is "doing the right thing," even when it requires sacrifice. Aspiring leaders can identify with this book, and not only deepen their own capabilities by reading it, but come to know an important final point about leadership: Not doing the wrong thing does not necessarily equal doing the right thing.

—Ross Perot
Founder, EDS and Perot Systems

At a time when integrity and leadership seem to have parted ways, Randy Pennington shows us a clear road back! This is an important book that should be read by everyone!

—Larry Winget
New York Times best-selling author of
*The Idiot Factor: The Ten Ways We
Sabotage Our Life, Money and Business*

I have spent 40 years in the Boy Scout movement, and 43 years in corporate America. I wondered when someone would make the connection. Randy did more than connect the dots, he provided a do-it-yourself plan for people to be ethical and successful.

—Roy S. Roberts
Past President, Boy Scouts of America
Retired Vice President and Group Executive of Marketing,
Sales and Service, General Motors Corporation
And a good scout for the rest of my life

This is a book that matters. However high the stack of business books sitting on your desk waiting to be read—read this one first. If we don't get this part right, nothing else will matter. Randy Pennington hasn't just given us a great business book, he has given us direction. This book helps us find true north.

—Joe Calloway
Author of *Becoming a Category of One*

Everyone should read this book. It reminds us, persuasively and substantively, that success without integrity is absolute failure in make-believe clothing. Randy Pennington is a top-notch author, speaker, and consultant. Highly recommended.

—Nido Qubein
President, High Point University
Chairman, Great Harvest Bread Company

Practical. Powerful. Essential. Randy has written the necessary book for organizations to thrive and create a "Thank God It's Monday" work environment where people thrive because the foundation is right.

—ROXANNE EMMERICH
New York Times best-selling author of *Thank God It's Monday*

Few individuals could summarize the principles of leadership and integrity in the straightforward manner in which Randy does. This real-world practical guide to success in business will not only mobilize the senior management of an organization to lead by example, but it will breed trust, accountability, and credibility throughout a company. As a result, employees and other constituents will become ambassadors with a drive for measurable results and success. Randy's book, while particularly timely in today's challenging environment, is, indeed, timeless.

—KURT DARROW
CEO, La-Z-Boy Corporation

Leaders need this book. In an age when easy and expedient trump integrity and virtue, Pennington's book is a refreshing reminder of what truly matters. His insights on enduring virtues and how to apply them to today's challenges are as relevant today as ever. Read it and share it with your team.

—MARK SANBORN
New York Times best-selling author of *The Fred Factor*
and *You Don't Need a Title to Be a Leader*

On My Honor, I Will is one of the best and most unique leadership books I have read. There are very few people who can articulate the importance of integrity in a leader's success any better than Randy Pennington. This book that is sorely needed today, and it will be even more important as we move into the future.

—KEITH WYCHE
President U.S. Operations
Pitney Bowes Management Services

On My Honor, I Will: The Journey to Integrity-Driven Leadership captures the essence of leadership. Leadership is based on relationships; relationships are based on trust; and trust is based on integrity. Integrity requires being honest with yourself and those you choose to influence. Pennington is right—Leadership is about <u>Your Honor</u>!

—KELLY S. KING
CEO, BB&T Financial Services

One of the problems I have with many books on leadership is that they are either all theories, with little regard to practical application—or, they are a biography of the CEO of some behemoth corporation that has little relevance to most of us. *On My Honor, I Will* is that rare and remarkable book that is both insightful and idealistic...practical while powerful...motivational with meaning. True leadership is always driven by integrity. *On My Honor, I Will* is an absolute knockout—and a MUST read!

—SCOTT MCKAIN
Vice Chairman, Obsidian Enterprises and
best-selling author of *Collapse of Distinction*

This is a unique book on leadership. Randy Pennington gives you real-life strategies to assess your values and integrity. Too many leadership books are vague and general. He proves that you can learn to be a leader at a different and higher level. You and your organization will be much better after reading and executing the ideas in this practical book.

—LISA FORD
Author of *How to Give Exceptional Customer Service*

In these times, the words honor and integrity carry an 'ouch' connotation for most of corporate America. Randy Pennington's book will help you understand why, while providing a game plan to build your corporate and personal integrity for a lifetime of success . . . Scout's honor.

— JEFFREY GITOMER
New York Times best-selling author of *The Little Red Book of Selling*

Randy Pennington's wisdom is what we need right now. He is leading the way toward a brand new leadership that offers time-tested solutions for a complex world.

—MARK A. RIECK
Executive Vice President,
International Right of Way Association

This powerful, inspiring book helps you to develop character, strength, and determination. You should read it and reread it again and again.

—BRIAN TRACY
Author of *Maximum Achievement*

Randy Pennington demonstrates how the Code of Conduct required by the Boy Scout Oath has, over more than a century, been prefigured and embodied by immortal leaders and peacemakers like Abraham Lincoln and Mahatma Gandhi. He argues persuasively that this code should guide and inspire persons of integrity who seek to lead our society today.

—ROBERT KRUEGER
U.S. Congressman, Senator, and Ambassador—and Eagle Scout

On My Honor, I Will is essential reading for anyone desiring to go beyond success and become significant as a leader. It will teach you to lead at a higher level and inspire you to become a better human being.

—DAVE ANDERSON
Author of *How to Run Your Business by THE BOOK:*
A Biblical Blueprint to Bless Your Business

Randy Pennington offers intriguing insights on leadership, integrity, and character development.

—RANDY GAGE
Author of *Prosperity Mind*

I quit Scouting about the same time as Randy for the same reasons. Just as he details so well in this book the basic tenets of Scouting can serve all of us very well as individuals and organizations. Through numerous examples, Randy highlights the best and worst in the area of individual and organizational integrity. I recommend this book as required reading for any CEO who wants his or her organization to thrive in an Integrity-Driven way.

—GARY L. NELON
Chairman/CEO First Texas Bancorp, Inc.

Integrity-based leadership and service to employees, customers, and society. What's not to love? The concept is so fundamental. Why don't we see more leaders exhibiting these behaviors? Pennington investigates the disconnect between our words and our actions and provides thoughtful insights into how to realign the two. A quick read that reminds you what being a leader is all about!

—TERRY PANKRATZ
Vice President for Finance and
CFO, Texas A&M University

Everyone knows that it is important to be an integrity-driven leader, but most do not know what that really means or how to do it. This book will lead you on a journey that describes, analyzes, and provides real-world examples of how to be integrity driven...regardless of the economic or social climate. If you will follow the principles outlined in this book, you will possess one of the most respected and valued virtues in life—integrity. Scout's Honor!

—DAVID COTTRELL
Author of *Monday Morning Choices*

On My Honor, I Will delivers a "character counts" message that is a must-read for anyone who wants to be a more effective leader. This is the stuff of greatness.

—BARRY SCHNEIDER
Managing Partner,
The Parkside Group LLC

ON MY
HONOR
I WILL

ON MY
HONOR
I WILL

THE JOURNEY TO
INTEGRITY-DRIVEN® LEADERSHIP

RANDY G. PENNINGTON

PenlandScott
PUBLISHERS

Dallas, Texas

Published by PenlandScott Publishers.

PenlandScott and colophon are trademarks of Red Honor Ventures, Ltd.

First Edition 2009

PenlandScott publications are available at special discounted rates for volume and bulk purchases, corporate and institutional premiums, promotions, fund-raising, and educational uses. For further information, contact:

PenlandScott Publishers
P.O. Box 166677
Irving, Texas 75016
specialsales@penlandscott.com

Front cover design by *the*BookDesigners.
Layout by Publications Development Company.

Printed and bound in the United States of America.

Library of Congress Control Number: 2009932480

ISBN-10: 0-9823-1521-X
ISBN-13: 978-0-9823-1521-7

Get informed & inspired at
www.penlandscott.com

10 9 8 7 6 5 4 3 2 1

To Mary—my partner in love and life—and to the Integrity-Driven Leaders who inspire us all.

THE BOY SCOUT OATH

On my honor I will do my best
To do my duty to God and my country
    and to obey the Scout Law;
To help other people at all times;
To keep myself physically strong,
    mentally awake, and morally straight.

—Boy Scouts of America,
Adopted 1911

THE GIRL SCOUT PROMISE

On my honor, I will try:
To serve God and my country,
To help people at all times,
And to live by the Girl Scout Law.

—Girl Scouts of the USA,
Adopted 1984
Used with permission

*The central need of our times is to find the road
we lost or abandoned, and to recover the values we
have rejected in favor of every man for himself in
pursuit of egoistic goals.*

—Laslo Nagy
Secretary-General,
World Organization of
the Scout Movement

HOW TO USE THIS BOOK

THIS BOOK IS A quick and easy read. The value, however, has less to do with the time it takes to complete and more to do with the time you take to think about and apply these lessons. Read the book at least twice. When you read it the first time, focus on the main theme and concepts. Then read it a second time to complete and think about the examples, exercises, and their application to your life and organization.

On My Honor, I Will can also serve as a guide for personal and/or organizational development. To use it in this way, do the following:

Identify specific areas for action and improvement based on your responses to the self-assessment at the end of Chapter 7.

Focus on one area of mastery at a time rather than working on all the concepts at once.

Set detailed goals for improvement, making sure to include the specific results you expect.

Track your performance and get feedback from others.

Spend time evaluating yourself and refining your performance.

An integrity-driven approach to leadership is a journey. There is no 5, 7, or 12-step program. You should return to the lessons in this book often. You will gain new understanding and perspective every time you read it. Happy learning and growing!

CONTENTS

THE BEGINNING

IT BEGAN WITH FIVE words: "He's a REAL BOY SCOUT."
Those were the words my client, Jim Horton, used to describe his boss. They were *not* meant as a compliment. Moments before, we had been at an impasse. Horton had hired us to provide consultation services for his firm. The project had gone well, and everyone was pleased. In fact, Horton had agreed to extend the scope of the agreement for an extra fee. Now, he was claiming that the extra work had been part of the original package, and he denied agreeing to any additional charges.

We *knew* we were right, and Horton *said* he was right. The old saying, "An unwritten agreement isn't worth the paper it's written on," came to mind. Without written evidence or corroborating testimony, we would be forced to accept Horton's account of the discussion.

"What about Mike Johnson?" I asked, remembering that Horton's manager had attended the meeting where the extra work had been discussed, priced, and approved.

The client gave a now-I've-got-you smile and picked up the phone. He buzzed his superior and asked him to join us. When Johnson arrived, Horton gave him the details of the dispute, making his own position perfectly clear.

Johnson listened carefully until his associate finished, then shook his head: "Oh, no, the consultant told us about the extra charge up front, and we both agreed it was fair. Don't you remember? In fact, you said the price was more than fair."

Horton mumbled something and thanked his supervisor. After Johnson left, Horton began shuffling papers on his desk. The awkward silence was broken by my associate, who said with relief, "I'm sure glad Mr. Johnson remembered."

Horton shook his head in disgust, "Yeah, he's a real Boy Scout."

✳   ✳   ✳

The story you have just read is true, although we have disguised the identity of the client and the exact situation. And although it occurred over 15 years ago, Horton's contention that honor and integrity are not consistent with long-term success concerned me then and continues to do so today.

MY SCOUTING PERSPECTIVE

I was a Boy Scout, although I never earned the rank of Eagle. Sports and other activities received more of my adolescent attention than Scouting, and I dropped out after earning the rank of First Class Scout. I always viewed the basement of the Kavanaugh Methodist Church as a place to hang out with my friends. Little did I know that between the games of four square, knot-tying competitions, and lessons about Native American life, the Scout Oath and Law were being drilled into my psyche.

I had no idea then that I would ever hear Boy Scout used as a disparaging moniker. Scouts in my hometown served as color guards for civic events, marched in parades, and went door-to-door collecting clothes or food for the needy.

Yet, here was a client in my grown-up world implying that the principle of doing what is right was archaic, outmoded, and fit only for children.

THE BAD NEWS

Horton was not alone in his beliefs then, and many others share his sentiments today. A quick scan of recent headlines indicates that there are many who continue to sacrifice honor, integrity, duty, and service at the altar of expedience. Some of them are elected officials, some of them are business leaders—and sadly, they seem to be everywhere.

Executives and evangelists have been punished for playing fast and loose with the money of others. Accounting standards have been manipulated to lock in corporate profits. Elected officials have been sanctioned (or worse) for violating ethical standards. Stockbrokers have been found guilty of insider trading. Leaders in government, business, entertainment, and sports have seen their careers tarnished for inappropriate behavior with subordinates, minors, and other assorted partners.

We're not talking about differences of opinion between people of honorable intention. These actions represent a blatant disregard for leading and living with integrity.

When Watergate conspirator Jeb Stuart Magruder was asked how he had sunk to such a despicable level, he hung his head and said, "I don't know. I guess I just lost my moral compass." Is the real or perceived loss of moral compass the reason for the high level of distrust and cynicism that exists in our society? Or is it merely the fact that bad news sells? Are we deep into a moral malaise, or are we held hostage by an instant and insatiable craving for news? Either way, it is imperative that leaders in all walks of life regain and maintain the mantle of honor and integrity that inspires others to follow.

HOW BAD IS IT?

James Patterson and Peter Kim provided a snapshot of our nation's views on leadership in their 1994 book *The Second American Revolution*.[1] According to their research, "two in three Americans don't believe we have any leaders with the ability to address the nation's ills; half of Americans don't have anyone in their family they'd like to model themselves after; and 70 percent of Americans believe our nation doesn't have heroes anymore."

A 2004 Reuters/DecisionQuest poll suggested that things haven't changed all that much.[2] Sixty-one percent of those surveyed indicated that their trust in leaders and institutions had declined between 2000 and 2004. In addition, those polled were asked to grade specific occupation groups on a scale of A+ (totally trustworthy) to F (failing). Perhaps these results match your feelings:

- Most democrats: C+

- Most state officials or politicians in your state: C

- Most newspaper reporters: C

- Most republicans: C

- Most television reporters: C

- Most U.S. senators and congressmen: C

- Most entertainment celebrities: C–

- Most lawyers: C–

- Most corporate executives: C–

A 2006 Lichtman/Zogby Interactive poll reported that only 3 percent of Americans think Congress is trustworthy.[3] Corporate leaders did not fare any better with only 7 percent categorized as trustworthy. Only 11 percent saw the media as deserving a high degree of trust.

This is not a purely American problem. A 2005 poll commissioned by the Canadian Broadcasting Company reported that nearly two-thirds of Canadians have little or no trust in their political leaders.[4] And a comparative study conducted by The Knesset Information Division in Israel found a worldwide problem with lack of trust in government institutions in general and parliaments in particular.[5]

Different studies conducted over 10 years apart in multiple parts of the world show similar results. Is this a coincidence? We think not.

Lack of trust is common. It destroys relationships and prevents people from working together to improve their situations. It doesn't matter if we are talking about governments, corporations, schools, religious institutions, or families.

THE GOOD NEWS

Horton's derogatory description of his boss led to the first edition of this book, co-authored with Marc Bockmon in 1992. Marc and I originally set out to send a strong message that traditional principles and values—like those articulated in the Boy Scout Oath and Girl Scout Promise—are critical for success in business and in life. If success is to be judged by column inches in the print media or feature stories on radio and television, we didn't achieve our goal.

Or did we? Since my early work with Marc, I have been privileged to learn from and present seminars to leaders throughout the world. I have seen firsthand that most leaders in all walks of life want to do the right thing. The principles espoused in the Scout Oath/Promise are widely known and accepted. Former Scouts make up a noticeable percentage of the corporate, association, and government audiences to which I speak. Many of the participants can recite the oath and law verbatim decades after their Scouting experiences.

This isn't a surprise. Scouting has been and continues to be known for character building and leadership development. The list of former Boy Scouts and Girl Scouts reads like a Who's Who that includes presidents, CEOs, astronauts, elected officials, sports and entertainment stars, and community leaders. Check out the people who volunteer their time, talents, and resources to Scouting and you will find the leaders in your community.

THE CYNICS AND DETRACTORS SPEAK

It doesn't happen often, but occasionally someone asks or comments about the stereotyped perceptions of people who support Scouting or reacts to the positions of Scouting organizations. The perception is that Scouts fit a certain mold and that they all agree on everything. My experience (and this is not an official statement from a Scouting organization) is that Scouts—like everyone else—share a diverse and sometimes opposite view of the world.

Do you think U.S. Presidents Gerald Ford and Jimmy Carter saw eye-to-eye on everything? How about Senator John Glenn and filmmaker Michael Moore? Or astronaut Neil Armstrong or rock star Jim Morrison of the Doors?

Former Secretary of Defense Donald Rumsfeld and Representative John "Jack" Murtha from Pennsylvania represented two distinct ends of argument on the U.S. war in Iraq. Both, like the other people listed here, are former Boy Scouts.

WHAT YOU WILL—AND WON'T—SEE IN THIS BOOK

Character building was a major goal of the Scouting movement from its beginning. In 1907, retired British General Sir Robert Baden-Powell, a war hero who had achieved national prominence, organized a camp for 22 boys. A year later, he published his first Boy Scout manual, and the movement swept England. In his book, *Scouting for Boys*, Baden-Powell proclaimed, "Scouting is a school of citizenship . . ."

Baden-Powell believed that good citizenship and leadership were uniquely connected. My goal is to show how traditional principles and values—like those articulated in the Boy Scout Oath—provide a blue-print for leadership that builds trust while achieving results.

In fact, the definition of Integrity-Driven® Leadership says it well: The art of influencing others to achieve results by leveraging the power of integrity and trust.

You will see stories, examples, and comments from a group of amazing leaders in all walks of life including H. Ross Perot, Rex Tillerson, Judge William S. Sessions, Mary Kay Ash, Howard Putnam, and Jose Niño. You will meet many others whose names may not be as familiar but who live and lead with integrity every day. My goal is to provide a diverse group of examples to show how you can influence others in a powerful and positive manner.

All leadership begins with *self-leadership,* so we provide suggestions that you can use where you are right now. Leadership, after all, is not about position but rather the ability—the passion and commitment—to influence others.

This book isn't about ideology and it is not about Scouting. This is a book about how to lead and live with integrity. Where political views or other multisided topics are discussed, every attempt is made to provide a balanced examination.

Although grounded in a strong sense of character, *On My Honor, I Will* is about more than ethics. Ethical intention without action toward a goal simply makes you feel better about achieving nothing. This book is about taking action.

> **It is common sense to take a method and try it. If it fails, admit it frankly and try another. But above all, try something.**
>
> *—Franklin D. Roosevelt*

THE NEW NEWS

One of cartoonist Gary Larson's classic *Far Side* comics shows a dinosaur behind a podium speaking to a group of his peers. The caption reads, "The picture is pretty bleak, gentlemen. The world's climates are changing, the mammals are taking over, and we all have a brain about the size of a walnut."

Like the cataclysmic changes that hastened the dinosaurs' extinction, we are facing a future that does not resemble the past in the way we live and work. In this world:

- **Everything is connected.** Advances in technology and communication enable us to be simultaneously and continuously in touch with anyone and everyone. But the connection goes much deeper. Thomas Friedman calls it the Dell Theory of Conflict Prevention: "No two countries that are both part of a major global supply chain, like Dell's, will ever fight a war against each other as long as they are both part of the same global supply chain."[6] Friedman acknowledges that his theory is not an absolute guarantee, but the premise is right on target. Our mutual success in every aspect of our lives is tied to the success of others . . . even people we have never met.

- **Communities are more than just the places we live.** Community used to be defined in geographic terms—neighborhoods, cities, states, or even countries. Now it is defined by areas of common interest. The scope of our interests and affiliations is unlimited. You may not know your neighbor although you may be intimately involved in the lives of friends and acquaintances around the world.

- **The lines between life away from work and life at work have blurred and in some cases disappeared.** Depending on your point of view and personal situation, this is either a good thing or a bad thing. Either way, it is a completely different way of interacting with the world and presents each of us with new challenges to find harmony in our lives and relationships.

- **Face-to-face interactions are becoming rarer.** Even though our world is more connected than ever, we can now live our lives without seeing anyone if we choose not to. Coworkers might reside in a different city, state, or country. You may never see your manager. For you, going to work might mean sitting down in front of a computer in a room in your house or apartment. Is this the norm? No, but it represents a trend in all aspects of society. You can purchase virtually any product or service without having to see—or in many cases, speak with—another person.

• **Engagement is a challenge for everyone.** Research done by the Gallup organization projects that the cost of employee disengagement is in the hundreds of billions of dollars.[7] This is just the tip of the iceberg in understanding the destructive nature of disengagement. What do we mean by disengagement? A disengaged citizenry doesn't bother to vote. Disengaged parents don't provide their children with the education and guidance they will need to lead productive lives; they do not participate in their children's sports activities or extra-curricular events. Disengaged leaders make careless decisions that affect others. Engaged citizens, parents, employees, teachers, communities, and leaders take a proactive interest in their success.

We need leaders who earn trust and credibility by their actions and interactions with others. We need leaders who can innovate to meet the challenges of change without selling out to the lure of shortcuts that place short-term return over long-term effectiveness. We need leaders who are concerned with doing what is right and who are not worried about who is right.

A UNIVERSAL MODEL FOR LEADERSHIP SUCCESS

In 1909, American businessman William Boyce became lost in the famous London fog while visiting England. A Boy Scout found him and, practicing the Scout slogan ("Do a good turn daily"), guided him to his appointment. Impressed, Boyce was determined to bring the Boy Scout movement to the United States. The following year, he succeeded. On

May 6, 1911, the Boy Scouts of America finalized their own Oath by adapting the model of their British counterparts.

On March 12, 1912, Juliette "Daisy" Gordon Low held the first Girl Scout meeting with 18 young women in Savannah, Georgia. Low had met Sir Robert Baden-Powell in 1911, and saw the importance of developing young women physically, mentally, and spiritually. Low returned to the United States to devote her energy to a new organization that would bring young women out of their home environments into the outdoors and promote community service.

Virtually nothing in America is the way it was in the early 1900s, yet through decades that brought boom and bust; recession and depression; wars and rumors of war; changes in transportation, communication, and lifestyles, the Scout Oath and the Scout Law have remained unchanged. They are intact for the same reason the Bill of Rights and other self-evident truths remain intact—because they work.

There are many models for being successful. Benjamin Franklin had his 13 virtues:

1. **Temperance:** Eat not to dullness; drink not to elevation.

2. **Order:** Let all your things have their places; let each part of your business have its time.

3. **Resolution:** Resolve to perform what you ought; perform without fail what you resolve.

4. **Frugality:** Make no expense but to do good to others or yourself; that is, waste nothing.

5. **Moderation:** Avoid extremes; forbear resenting injuries so much as you think they deserve.

6. **Industry:** Lose no time; be always employed in something useful; cut off all unnecessary actions.

7. **Cleanliness:** Tolerate no uncleanliness in body, clothes, or habitation.

8. **Tranquility:** Be not disturbed at trifles or at accidents common or unavoidable.

9. **Silence:** Speak not but what may benefit others or yourself; avoid trifling conversation.

10. **Sincerity:** Use no hurtful deceit; think innocently and justly, and, if you speak, speak accordingly.

11. **Justice:** Wrong none by doing injuries or omitting the benefits that are your duty.

12. **Chastity:** Rarely use venery but for health or offspring, never to dullness, weakness, or the injury of your own or another's peace or reputation.

13. **Humility:** Imitate Jesus and Socrates.[8]

Sam Walton had his 10 rules for being a success in business:

1. **Commit** to your business.

2. **Share** your profits with all your associates and treat them as partners.

3. **Motivate** your partners.

4. **Communicate** everything you possibly can to your partners.

5. **Appreciate** everything your associates do for the business.

6. **Celebrate** your successes.

7. **Listen** to everyone in your company.

8. **Exceed** your customers' expectations.

9. **Control** your expenses better than your competition.

10. **Swim** upstream.[9]

J. Paul Getty proposed a three-step approach that many find useful:

> *Rise early.*
> *Work hard.*
> *Strike oil.*

There is, however, no better model for success as a leader, whatever your walk of life, than the forty words that make up the Scout Oath.[10] They form the roadmap for the journey to Integrity-Driven Leadership:

> *On my honor I will do my best*
> *To do my duty to God and my country*
> *and to obey the Scout Law;*
> *To help other people at all times;*
> *To keep myself physically strong,*
> *mentally awake, and morally straight.*

Robert Mazucca, Chief Scout for the Boy Scouts of America, put it this way during an interview with Matthew Kirdahy of *Forbes* magazine:

> *People who come through scouting know that the principles we*
> *work with are really valuable principles. If you want to be a*
> *good parent, just live by the scout oath and law. You want to be*
> *a good employee, live by the scout oath and law. You want to be a*
> *good CEO, live by the scout oath and law.*[11]

You have heard or repeated these forty words before. Let's look at them again from a leadership perspective:

On my honor I will: A keen sense of ethical conduct. My word is given as my bond to do what I say I will do. ~~Not "I might,"~~ or "I'll think about it." You can count on me. I am committed.

Do my best: I will go beyond what's required to meet the minimum standards. You will receive my best performance and effort every day.

To do my duty: I will do what's right even when it is not convenient or pleasant.

To God and my country: I understand and accept my responsibilities that go beyond my selfish desires. I answer to a power that is higher than a quick profit.

And to obey the Scout Law: I will be trustworthy, loyal, helpful, friendly, courteous kind, obedient, cheerful, thrifty, brave, clean, and reverent in all areas of my life.

To help other people at all times: I influence others through a sense of service regardless of their position or mine.

To keep myself physically strong, mentally awake, and morally straight: My responsibility for my health enables me to perform more effectively. I will remain mentally awake and anticipate the changing expectations of my world, and I embrace the fact that the trust of others must be earned through my leadership example.

WILL THIS BOOK CHANGE YOUR MIND OR BEHAVIOR?

Great question. The answer is "Yes," "No," and "Maybe."

The old saying goes, "I'll believe it when I see it." The examples provided in this book paint a compelling picture, and if you take an honest look, they offer a time-tested model for success as a leader.

Of course, the converse is true as well: "I'll see it when I believe it."

There will be those who allow their preconceived beliefs to prevent them from gaining any perspectives or insights that could improve their lives. If you fall into this category, this book—or any book—is unlikely to provide you with anything beneficial.

Then there are those who will dismiss the very premise of this book as outdated and simplistic. I disagree with them. I agree that we face complex challenges in our families, communities, workplaces, and world.

We need new thinking and the ability to build partnerships with others. Albert Einstein was correct: "The problems that exist in the world today cannot be solved by the level of thinking that created them." But I believe that while tools and ideas change, evolve, and innovate, principles remain constant.

The principles discussed here are simple to understand and incredibly difficult to implement. In a world where change and complexity are the order of the day, I propose that we need a common—and, yes, simple—set of principles to guide us as leaders.

The "Maybe" answer holds out hope that you will internalize this message and decide to do something different.

This book is merely a catalyst. We can't bring about internal change with external medicine. In fact, applying an external solution to an internal problem is like taking morphine for cancer. It may disguise the symptoms, but it doesn't do anything to cure the disease.

> **Start by doing what's necessary, then what's possible, and suddenly you are doing the impossible.**
>
> —*St. Francis of Assisi*

So in the end, this book is like many others. It can be useful or not depending on you and your actions. To genuinely increase our organizational and individual success, the change must come from within. This takes more time and effort, but it brings lasting change. It's the kind of change that shifts the focus from *who* is right to *what* is right. Then and only then can we be truly successful.

IT USED TO WORK . . .

People once helped each other build homes and raise barns. There was a time when an honest person could borrow money at the bank on a handshake. The beauty of the Scout Oath and Law is that they're like gravity—they work whether you believe in them or not. Oh, you can get away with ignoring these principles for a while—but in the end you lose the trust and respect of others that is necessary for success in today's interdependent world.

. . . AND IT STILL CAN

I readily admit that the idea of everyone living their lives based on traditional principles such as honor, integrity, duty, and service is at best a pipe dream. As you will see, even the people who are committed to leading and living this way struggle from time to time. I certainly do.

So here is my question to you: Can you be better at modeling these principles tomorrow than you were today? You don't have to be a bad parent to want to be a better parent. You don't have to be unhealthy to want to be healthier. And, you don't have to be dishonorable to want to live and lead with more honor.

I'm not asking for much. Just consistent effort, the realization that living and leading with integrity is a journey with successes and failures rather than a series of easy-to-implement steps, and the hope that you—like me—won't be offended if someone calls you a "real Boy Scout."

CHAPTER TWO

──── ✳ ────

LEADERSHIP

What Does Integrity Have to Do with It?

*The principles of leadership are timeless because
even in a rapidly changing world, human nature
remains a constant.*

—H. Ross Perot

THE DRIVER BROUGHT THE automobile to a complete stop at the stop
sign and looked both ways.

"Why are you stopping? We're in the middle of nowhere, and no one
is watching to make sure you stopped at this stop sign?"

My father looked at my mother and then nodded to my brother and
me in the backseat. "There are four eyes in the backseat watching."

Family, friends, coworkers, and strangers on the street watch us. Our
bosses take notice and use their perceptions to determine our effectiveness. So do employees, customers, and vendors.

We are given names by others to describe their perceptions and beliefs about our performance and behavior. If you don't pull your weight
or do what you said you would do, then your bosses call you a slacker or
perhaps use the more polite term "disengaged."

Don't play nice in the sandbox with your coworkers, and you are
labeled as eccentric or perhaps as someone with a bad attitude.

Fail to follow through on commitments, and your coworkers call you dead weight . . . or something worse. Behave this way at home, and your family calls you unloving; uncaring; a bad parent, spouse, partner, or child.

Set a great example of performance and commitment—do what you say you will, be trustworthy, and live for a purpose higher than your own—and they'll call you a leader.

WHAT IS LEADERSHIP?

Leaders influence people through what they say, what they do, and how they say and do it. Leadership has nothing to do with position and everything to do with your ability to convince others to act—sometimes against their own immediate interests—to accomplish a goal or task. That makes leadership the factor that distinguishes you in every aspect of your life.

> **If your actions inspire others to dream more, learn more, do more, and become more, you are a leader.**
>
> —*John Quincy Adams*

Every leader is concerned about results. Some leaders use their position to influence your actions and outcomes. Others use their personal performance to set an example. Some lead through fear. Others rely on a reputation of service and trustworthiness.

By obeying the law and coming to a complete stop when no one was looking, my father was leading by example. And the coworker or team member who influences others through her actions and language—either positive or negative—is practicing leadership, too.

INTEGRITY, PORNOGRAPHY, AND LEADERSHIP

"I know it when I see it." Supreme Court Justice Potter Stewart's 1964 explanation of when pornography crosses the line to obscenity has become "one of the most famous phrases in the entire history" of the Supreme Court.[1] And, it has become the response of choice when describing a subjective fact, event, or characteristic.

Which brings us to integrity. We know integrity is important. It appears at or near the top of every list of desirable leadership traits. We claim it as the mantle of the politicians with whom we agree and decry its absence in those with whom we disagree.

Rex Tillerson, CEO of Exxon Mobil Corporation told me, "You can be brilliant in your profession, but if you don't have honor and integrity, there won't be a place for you. If you ever compromise those, you'll never be successful."

So how do you define integrity? Go ahead—take a stab at it. Integrity is . . .

It is more difficult to define integrity than you thought, isn't it? And that is the challenge: How can you live and lead with integrity if you can't clearly define it?

For many people, *integrity* is synonymous with ethics. That's a critical piece of it, but there is more to it than that. A computer program has integrity when it does what it is designed to do without errors. A computer disk has integrity when it is free of defects and is operating properly. A building has integrity when its construction meets all the required standards. Art has integrity when it is pure and consistent with the artist's vision.

Legendary singer and songwriter Willie Nelson was asked if his life philosophy had changed at the age of 75. Willie responded, "No. When I go back and listen to those early songs I've written and listen to the ones I've written yesterday, I still have basically the same beliefs that everything is good."[2] That, too, is integrity.

LEADERSHIP ISN'T A POSITION

Henry Givray is Chairman and CEO of SmithBucklin Corporation, the largest association management and professional services company in the world. Does that automatically make him a leader?

By most standards, the answer is "Yes." Like all CEOs, his job is to set the direction, monitor progress, and ensure that results are delivered. But by Givray's standards, the answer is "No!"

"It's not for me to say that I am a leader," says Givray. "Leadership is not something that is bestowed upon you or granted to you by virtue of your title or position. In fact, leadership is invited and can only be given willingly by others based on who you are and what you do, and it is revealed by what you inspire and what you enable."

CEOs possess strong skills in strategy development, finance, and negotiation, but leaders are shaped and defined by character," says Givray. "CEOs measure success in terms of earnings, market share growth, and stock price appreciation. Leaders measure success through the success of all of those they serve, including customers, employees, shareholders, and communities—and they live by a fundamental tenet—that service to others is one of the highest honors and greatest obligations of a leader."

The differences are more than semantics. The position of CEO—or any other position of power—provides the leverage to mandate certain performance. Givray believes that leaders have a higher calling: to visualize a better future state, inspire others to join the journey, and enable success in getting there.

The ability to inspire and enable others, Givray believes, stems from certain distinguishing, nonnegotiable qualities. These include uncompromised integrity, courage to do the right thing (rather than what is expedient, popular, or personally beneficial), and an unyielding pledge to put service to others ahead of self-interest.

Givray worked at SmithBucklin between 1983 and 1996. Prior to rejoining SmithBucklin as its CEO in 2002, he served as CEO of a successful online legal services start-up during the dot-com boom and bust periods. In 2001, it was clear that taking his company public and reaping the rewards of an initial public offering (IPO) were not in the cards. Not to be discouraged, Givray negotiated a deal with LexisNexis to acquire his company.

The terms of the deal were negotiated and delivered to the board for approval. Included, by the buyer, was a sale price that included a $1 million stipend to Givray to ensure that he would remain committed, energetic, and enthusiastic to make the transaction a reality. Givray's board recognized his accomplishments and approved the million-dollar payment. His executive team said, "You deserve this!"

Givray knew the sale was the right thing to do for his employees, his customers, and for the stockholders. But receiving the stipend didn't feel right. The $1 million was coming at the expense of the stockholders. And the buyer's purpose in providing it—to keep Givray motivated and energized—wasn't achieving its goal.

The night the board approved the deal including the $1 million stipend, Givray went home and told his wife about his dilemma. Frankly, he could use the money—the collapse of the IPO markets had rendered his stock options worthless. He was at a low point in terms of his financial assets. The next morning, Givray announced to the board that he was giving back the $1 million stipend so that it could go to the stockholders.

In 2005, three years after returning to SmithBucklin as its CEO, Givray led the transfer of ownership from financial investors to its employees. The decision was a natural extension of the company's pledge to take care of people so that they can take care of clients. Under SmithBucklin's Employee Stock Ownership Plan (ESOP), every employee regardless of position, compensation, or tenure has an equal opportunity to acquire ownership in the company.

Givray admits that as CEO he would have received a larger ownership stake and made more money personally if the company had been sold to another set of financial investors rather than going the ESOP route with its employees. Driving Givray's decision to pursue this particular type of ESOP was his deeply held belief that SmithBucklin employees, not outsiders, create value for clients and the company. And since employees control the company's destiny, they should have the opportunity to experience the fulfillment and reap the rewards of ownership. Givray says that the transfer of ownership from outsiders to his employees on an equal and fair basis was by far the proudest moment in his career.

Some will say that Givray didn't have to walk away—or in fact, shouldn't have walked away—from personal financial gain that could have justly rewarded his performance. After all, taking the money in either situation would have been perfectly acceptable and in line with any standard of business risk and rewards. For Givray, it comes back to that fundamental tenet: "service to others is one of the highest honors and greatest obligations of a leader." To do anything else would have violated his personal sense of integrity and doing what was right.

SmithBucklin is on a journey to build a great, enduring company. That is the overarching, better future state that Givray envisions. It's no surprise that

Givray's articulated 10 measures of SmithBucklin greatness all tie specifically to the present and future interests of clients, employees, and stakeholders. He knows that the passion and unrelenting dedication of the SmithBucklin people to their clients and to the company will create boundless opportunities. He told me, "Measuring success through the success of all of those I serve will achieve superlative, sustainable results not only for my constituents but for me as well."

Leadership is recession proof," says Givray. "It is the one imperative above all else that enables everything else within an organization and its people—focus and flexibility, agility and speed, strategic thinking and action taking, innovation and boldness, passion and commitment, resilience and hardiness, and alignment and cohesiveness—in good times and in bad."[3]

✴

INTEGRITY DEFINED

Webster's *New World Dictionary* defines integrity as, "the quality or state of being complete; wholeness; the quality or state of being unimpaired; and being of sound moral principle."

Still a little unclear? Perhaps breaking down Webster's definition in practical terms will help. Seven themes emerge when the dictionary definition of integrity is applied to how we live and lead. Think of them as the Seven Cs of Integrity:

1. **Clarity:** Individuals who act with integrity are clear on their values, beliefs, and priorities. Like a fine gemstone, light shined on this person is not scattered or diffused by impurities and inconsistencies. Clarity of purpose and principles are evident in every action, decision, and communication.

2. **Constancy:** Faithfulness, fidelity, stability, steadfast, and unwavering—these are the words that define the person who possesses constancy. She is unwavering in her dedication. He is steadfast in

his beliefs. They are faithful to the commitments and promises they make. There is a fine line between constancy and rigidity. Constancy—and by connection integrity—does not shackle you to a set of beliefs forever. It requires thoughtful examination to determine the truth.

3. **Consistency:** Closely tied to constancy, consistency transforms beliefs into action. The constancy of our beliefs is demonstrated through the consistency of our actions. Consistency promotes trust and provides a sense of stability to others.

4. **Congruency:** Congruency in geometry means that two objects are roughly the same shape and size. Applied to people, it means there is consistency between what we feel on the inside and what we do on the outside. Congruency takes the concept of consistency to a deeper level. You can be consistent without being congruent. But, you cannot be congruent without being consistent.

5. **Commitment:** Commitment requires two things: a promise and an involvement. The person of integrity commits or pledges to act in a specific manner. A commitment is articulated in the Scout Oath through two words: I will. The promise obligates involvement. The pledge to do your duty is merely a statement of intention without the active engagement and action. As the pig said to the chicken at the suggestion that they treat their caretaker farmer to a breakfast of ham and eggs, "This requires your participation. I, on the other hand, am making a commitment."

6. **Courage:** Courage is the willingness to face or deal with anything that is dangerous, difficult, or painful rather than avoiding it by making another choice. From a physical sense, it is an example of the fight/flight decision. Do you confront the

thing you fear or do you flee for safety? The implication holds true from a moral perspective. The person of integrity faces and makes the difficult choice even when the outcome could be painful or unpopular.

7. **Concern:** Concern when used as a verb means to show interest or regard for a person or thing. Its opposite is indifference. The concern we speak of here is what Webster defined as a "sound moral principle." It is the ethical part of the definition of integrity. The person of integrity is concerned with understanding and doing what's right. Concern also requires consideration of others' interests rather than a sole devotion to our own.

THAT'S INTERESTING—SO WHAT?

It takes 460 words to explain the definition of a word we all believe that we know and understand. That's the point. We don't all share the same definition of a word that is universally considered an important trait for all leaders to have. You might believe that integrity is consistency. I might see it as congruency or courage. We would both be right, and neither of us would be any closer to a common understanding of what it takes to live and lead with integrity.

So here is my definition of integrity: Completeness, honesty, and transparency in thought, communication, and action.

Integrity means being accountable and responsible not just to yourself, but to also consider the implications of actions and decisions on others—ethically, morally, and physically. It means being clear, constant, and consistent in the beliefs and values for which you stand. Integrity means that there is congruency between internal beliefs and external actions. And it means that you have the courage to do what's right even when it is not convenient or no one else is looking.

INTEGRITY REQUIRES ALL SEVEN Cs

Did Adolf Hitler have integrity as a leader? This is a question that always spurs vigorous debate. Hitler had clarity in his beliefs, values, and priorities. He consistently displayed constancy of belief. You could argue that Hitler demonstrated congruency, commitment, and courage. But when evaluating integrity in leadership, Hitler failed miserably.

Pulitzer Prize–winning author, James MacGregor Burns noted, "Hitler, once he gained power and crushed all opposition, was no leader—he was a tyrant. A leader and a tyrant are polar opposites."[4]

Burns makes the important distinction between leaders and people who merely wield power. All leaders have power, but not everyone with power is a leader. He goes on to say, "Much of what commonly passes as leadership—conspicuous position-taking without followers or follow-through, posturing on various public stages, manipulation without general purpose, authoritarianism—is no more leadership than the behavior of small boys marching in front of a parade, who continue to strut along Main Street after the procession has turned down a side street toward the fair grounds."[5]

CONCERN—THE VITAL INGREDIENT

Burns answers the question of Hitler's (or any other tyrant's) integrity with this description:

> *Adolf Hitler would argue that he spoke the true values of the German people, summoned them to a higher destiny, evoked the noblest sacrifice from them. The most crass, favor-swapping politician can point to the followers he helps or satisfies . . . Both Hitler and the politician would have to be tested by the modal values of honor and integrity—by the extent to which they advanced or thwarted fundamental standards of good conduct in humankind.*[6]

I recognize the obvious contradiction—and potential risks—in using Hitler as a discussion point in a book about leadership integrity. My purpose is not to offend. Hitler is simply the most recognizable name in a list of tyrants throughout history who have attempted to cloak themselves in the trappings of honor and integrity without actually having either of those qualities because they lacked a sense of concern.

Concern is an interest in others and doing what's right based on sound moral character. It is the factor that separates the integrity-driven leader from the little boy marching in front of the parade or the tyrant seeking power for the sake of personal reward.

HISTORY RELIVED TODAY

Dr. Jim Tunney is remembered by professional football fans in the United States as the dean of NFL referees. His distinguished 31-year career landed him in the NFL Hall of Fame. But, Dr. Tunney is also an educator with 28 years of experience as a teacher, coach, principal, school superintendent, and member of the board of trustees at both the high school and college level. In his work as an educator, Dr. Tunney had significant experience working with inner-city gangs and gang leaders.

The only test of leadership is that somebody follows.

—*Robert K. Greenleaf*

When asked about the differences and similarities between the gang leaders and the student body presidents with whom he has worked, Tunney told me, "I believe that the leadership characteristics between a gang leader and the school's student body president are often similar. However, the gang leader leads his followers toward a negative, often destructive, environment while the student body president influences his followers toward a positive healthy environment."

Both history and current experience prove that the leader without a sound moral character and concern for others will be abandoned at the first sign of difficulty. Tunney says, "When there are character flaws in the individual leader, all too often the old CYA philosophy rises up when the pressure is on. The followers are quick to turn against the leader."

HOW INTEGRITY-DRIVEN LEADERS EARN POWER

As we noted earlier, all great leaders expect results. They create focus with clear goals and high expectations. They ensure effective execution of well-designed strategies. Integrity-driven leaders approach their leadership responsibilities from a different perspective.

Power, for integrity-driven leaders, comes from trust rather than fear. It is earned through the strength of their character, the clarity of their communication, the honesty of their relationships, the courage of their commitments, and the consistency and congruency of their actions and performance. Integrity-driven leaders generate confidence and commitment rather than skepticism and cynicism.

Why is that important? What would be different in your organization if every individual could be trusted to act with integrity? From a business perspective, what might you be able to save in compliance costs? What might you be able to achieve through increased productivity and performance? How might a reputation for integrity in products, services, and relationships affect customer loyalty?

> **If everyone were clothed with integrity, if every heart were just, frank, kindly, the other virtues would be well-nigh useless.**
>
> —*Molière [Jean-Baptiste Poquelin] Tartuffe, V, i*

What would be different in your friendships, relationships, and family? Most of the examples in this book will be taken from business, but the concepts apply to other areas as well. There is no "business life and home life." There is only "life," and the way we lead it matters.

INTEGRITY, HONOR, AND RESULTS

Barry Schneider founded The Parkside Group in 1997 following the sale of his company MSA Industries to E.I. DuPont de Nemours & Company. During the preceding decade, Schneider transformed MSA Industries from a small family-owned business with annual sales of $4 million into the largest distributor and service provider of commercial floor coverings in the United States. By the time MSA Industries was sold to DuPont, it had become the industry's leader, with 46 branches in 31 states generating in excess of $300 million in annual revenue. For the final three years under Schneider's leadership, the company grew at a 63 percent compounded annual growth rate.

Surely a tough-minded business leader like Schneider believes in results at any cost.

Actually, Schneider believes that "too many leaders today have become obsessed with output. We've become a slave to quarter-to-quarter results. Shareholder value is a long-term notion, and we need to treat it that way."

Schneider says, "Respect and integrity don't need spin doctors."

Ralph Waldo Emerson said it another way,

The louder he spoke of his honor, the faster we counted our spoons.

We live in a world where trust, confidence, and credibility are the victims of the quest for success at any cost. We are skeptical, and often cynical, about the motives behind the actions of others. We have witnessed a lack of integrity in our elected officials, heroes, and even in the institutions on which we rely to define our society. Integrity lapses are not confined to business and the workplace. Examples can be drawn from our schools, government, religion, and even families.

Schneider knows that velocity is a key differentiator in the success of his company and the companies in which he invests. He has to move quickly to capture opportunities, and he needs the people with whom he works to do the same. That doesn't happen without the trust that comes from honor, integrity, transparency, and respect.

He puts it this way, "Integrity is about fulfilling a commitment, even when doing so is agaisnt one's self-interest. Integrity naturally leads to trust and credibility, and when applied consistently throughout an organization, drives high velocity execution and dealmaking . . . which is a huge competitive advantage." Schneider's formula is simple:

Honor and Integrity + a Good Business Model = Superior Execution

There is no shortage of good business models or strategies. Business savvy is a fundamental expectation. It is the ticket to get in the game, but it will not ensure long-term success on the field of play.

Your success as a leader—regardless of your position or the endeavor—is magnified when you are known as a person of honor and integrity.

HOW ABOUT YOU?

Do you embody the seven characteristics that define integrity? All the time? Regardless of the situation? Complete the assessment that follows to determine how you are doing. The survey is not scientific, but it is a strong indicator of your commitment to integrity as a leader. And, like every survey, the validity of your answers is in direct proportion to the honesty of your responses.

Rate yourself on a scale of 1 to 5 with 5 being *Excellent* and 1 being *Needs Improvement.*

1. I know what I stand for. There is clarity in my values, priorities, and goals. ____

2. I make decisions based on what's right for all parties and not on the basis of tradition, expediency, or political positioning. ____

3. I have a reputation of honesty and trustworthiness with those with whom I have a relationship. _____

4. Telling the truth is rewarded. I don't shoot messengers or avoid the truth to protect the illusion of success. _____

5. I stand up for the principles in which I believe—even when it is not convenient. _____

6. I am consistent and congruent in thoughts, actions, words, and deeds. _____

7. I honor commitments and promises and do what I say I will do. _____

8. I am open and transparent in my dealings with others. I do not hide information that should be shared with others. _____

9. I help other people and operate from a sense of service. _____

10. I consider the moral and ethical implications of my decisions and actions rather than doing what is convenient or expedient at the time. _____

Total _____

Scoring

- If you scored 40 or above, congratulations! You understand and embrace the importance of integrity as a leader. There may be a few areas you want to fine-tune, but you are doing well. The remainder of this book will serve as a great reminder as well as provide some new perspectives to consider.

- If you scored between 30 and 40, you're doing a good job overall, but there are probably a few specific areas on which you should work. Make a few notes now about the areas on which you need to work. Start with those areas where you rated yourself a 1 or 2. Then move to the areas where you rated yourself as a 3. Describe what you would be thinking and doing differently if you were acting as the leader you want to become. Doing so will help you be more focused and receptive as you complete this book.

- If you scored below 30, it is time to take immediate action. Spend some time in self-reflection to determine your commitment to integrity as a tool to interact with and influence others. Seek honest feedback from others you trust. And take time at the end of each remaining chapter within this book to create an action plan. Your efforts will be appreciated, and you will become a more effective leader.

WHAT'S NEXT?

Did you score a perfect 50 on your assessment? The leaders who are truly honest with themselves never do. They understand that the journey toward integrity-driven leadership never ends. The closer they come to a perfect score, the more they realize there is always more to learn and do.

Leadership occurs at three levels: Individual, Interpersonal, and Organizational (see Figure 2.1). The next three chapters of this book provide specific actions you can take in each of these leadership levels to continue your journey toward integrity-driven leadership. The link between the Individual, Interpersonal, and Organizational aspects of leadership is crucial. The organizational integrity lapses that populate the headlines always begin with individual and interpersonal integrity lapses.

The last two chapters deal with application and change. We will draw connections between the challenges and dilemmas that make headlines and the routine, but no less difficult, issues you and I face each day. We'll examine ways to build an integrity-driven culture that produces a generation of leaders who embrace the belief that true power comes from a position of credibility, trust, and service.

Figure 2.1 Three Levels of Leadership

If your idea of a successful leader is someone who looks out only for himself or herself and aspires to influence through manipulation, coercion, and threat, you may not enjoy this book. Then again, you probably did not make it this far. You do need to continue reading, however. The expectations for leaders are changing. Leadership is no longer an automatic reward of position.

Integrity-driven leadership is hard work, but the payoff is the credibility to influence others even when you are no longer around them every day. The eyes in the backseat are always watching as we continue the journey. Let's get started.

CHAPTER THREE

MASTER THE DISCIPLINE
OF PERSONAL INTEGRITY

Character is destiny.

—HERACLITES

B RONZE STATUES . . . 15 OF them . . . young children of approximately the same age running, kicking soccer balls, chasing butterflies, and being . . . children.

This was hardly the image I anticipated as I crossed the atrium bridge that led to the office of H. Ross Perot, the billionaire founder of EDS and Perot Systems, and a two-time presidential candidate. This is the man who financed and orchestrated the daring rescue of his employees from a prison in Iran and became the subject of the book and TV mini-series *On Wings of Eagles*. This man is an icon, and the first things you see are statues of children? Surely they were the collected works of a world-renowned sculptor.

"I like your statues," my companion said.

Perot's face lit up like a fireworks finale on the Fourth of July. "Those are my grandchildren. I get to see them every day."

As he escorted us into his office, the importance of Perot's comments immediately became clear. Memorabilia from his family covered space on every wall. From photos and portraits of his wife and children to the ledger page taken from his father's business, the influence of and devotion to family surrounded us.

At the end of our time together, Perot showed us his copy of the U.S. Constitution on display just outside of his office. And he pointed out the restored 1929 Dodge automobile driven by his family and the bronze statue of a horse carrying his father's saddle in the lobby below. A pair of his father's boots completed the testimony of this man's influence on Perot's life.

Love of family and country that drives unquestioned duty and devotion. The signs were everywhere, and to view them puts the life and leadership of H. Ross Perot into crystal clear perspective. Clarity is easy when you witness personal integrity.

WHAT DID WE TALK ABOUT?

Perot and I spoke for almost 60 minutes about leadership—some of it his and most of it others'. I learned that Perot's mother and father modeled service and generosity, helping others. Growing up during the Great Depression, his house was a regular stopping point for hobos traveling through his hometown. Learning that their house had been "marked" as a place where a helping hand would be offered, Perot offered to remove the mark on the curb in front of their house. His mother responded, "No, son, leave it there. These are good people. They are just like us, but they are down on their luck. We should help them."

Perot spent time every day with his father, often riding horses together from the time he completed his school day until dark. He had been told that a Boy Scout could earn the rank of Eagle Scout in 13 months, and Perot learned the value of goal setting by doing so. He spoke of Josh Morris Jr. the young man from his neighborhood who inspired him to gain admittance to the Naval Academy, and he spoke at length about the leadership of Colonel Arthur D. "Bull" Simons in orchestrating the rescue of two EDS employees from an Iranian prison.

When asked why he undertook the rescue rather than let the U.S. government negotiate a resolution, Perot credited his mother who told him, "These are your men. You sent them over there. It is your responsibility to get them out."

I walked into my conversation admiring H. Ross Perot. But, admiration is not understanding. I walked away understanding that mastering the discipline of personal integrity requires each of us to live the following five principles in every aspect of our lives:

1. **Know** what you stand for.

2. **Serve** a cause greater than yourself.

3. **Follow** your core in good times and bad.

4. **Set** goals and deliver your best performance.

5. **Live** positively.

THE POWER OF PURPOSE

Dr. Viktor Frankl lost virtually everything in the Nazi concentration camps during World War II. His father, mother, wife, and brother perished in the camps. Every possession was taken from him. Frankl was stripped physically and emotionally to the naked existence of survival. His sister was his only surviving family member.

> **Behind every goal you set for yourself, there will be some value or cluster of values.**
>
> *—Tom Morris, Ph.D.*

In the Preface to Frankl's book, influential psychologist Gordon Allport wrote, "In the concentration camp, every circumstance conspires to make the prisoner lose his hold. All of the familiar goals are snatched away."[1]

Dr. Frankl noted that "only the men that allowed their inner hold on their moral and spiritual selves to subside eventually fell victim to the camp's degenerating influences."[2] When you lose your sense of purpose—what you stand for—you are doomed to decline and decay. The prisoners who lost their hold in the concentration camp believed that there was nothing more to expect from life. Frankl rejected that notion and focused on what life expected from him.[3]

For Frankl, the sense of purpose included the things he wanted or was compelled to accomplish in the future. His professional training and concentration camp experience led him to develop Logotherapy, a form of existential analysis that made him one of the leading thinkers in psychotherapy along with Sigmund Freud and Alfred Adler. He devoted his professional life to helping people embrace the power of meaning in their lives. Frankl authored 32 books published in 32 languages, lectured at 209 universities, and received honorary doctorate degrees from 29 universities.

For Perot, that sense of purpose includes faith, family, and duty. For the integrity-driven leader, a sense of purpose and meaning forms the foundation from which all decisions are made.

HOW ABOUT YOU?

What is at your core? What is the sense of purpose and meaning to which you hold when faced with the worst circumstance imaginable? Core beliefs must be identified before they can be followed.

Your situation will hopefully never rival Frankl's concentration camp experience, but there are always challenges. And it is there that the discipline of personal integrity separates the leaders from everyone else.

Dr. Sidney B. Simon wrote a book titled *In Search of Values*. In it, he provides 31 exercises to identify the principles and values that really matter in your life. My favorite is called "The Eulogy." The task is straightforward: Write the eulogy you would like delivered after your death.[4]

Before you dismiss this as a morbid activity with little relevance, consider that the eulogy we would want delivered reflects the truest aspirations for our lives.

EULOGIES THAT REFLECT INTEGRITY

The light has gone out, I said, and yet I was wrong. For the light that shone in this country was no ordinary light. The light that has illumined this country for these many years will illumine this country for many more years, and a thousand years later that light will still be seen in this country, and the world will see it and it will give solace to innumerable hearts. For that light represented the living truth . . . the eternal truths, reminding us of the right path, drawing us from error, taking this ancient country to freedom.

FROM JAWAHARIAL NEHRU'S EULOGY FOR MOHANDAS
KARAMCHAND (MAHATMA) GANDHI

Others saw only limits to growth; he transformed a stagnant economy into an engine of opportunity.

Others hoped, at best, for an uneasy cohabitation with the Soviet Union; he won the Cold War—not only without firing a shot, but also by inviting enemies out of their fortress and turning them into friends.

I cannot imagine how any diplomat, or any dramatist, could improve on his words to Mikhail Gorbachev at the Geneva summit: "Let me tell you why it is we distrust you." Those words are candid and tough and they cannot have been easy to hear. But they are also a clear invitation to a new beginning and a new relationship that would be rooted in trust.

We live today in the world that Ronald Reagan began to reshape with those words. It is a very different world with different challenges and new dangers. All in all, however, it is one of greater freedom and prosperity, one more hopeful than the world he inherited on becoming president.

FROM LADY MARGARET THATCHER'S EULOGY FOR RONALD REAGAN

I'm here today to say a final thank you, Sister Rosa, for being a great woman who used your life to serve, to serve us all. That day that you refused to give up your seat on the bus, you, Sister Rosa, changed the trajectory of my life and the lives of so many other people in the world. I would not be standing here today nor standing where I stand every day had she not chosen to sit down. I know that. I know that. I know that. I know that, and I honor that. Had she not chosen to say we shall not—we shall not be moved.

So I thank you again, Sister Rosa, for not only confronting the one white man whose seat you took, not only confronting the bus driver, not only for confronting the law, but for confronting history, a history that for 400 years said that you were not even worthy of a glance, certainly no consideration. I thank you for not moving.

And in that moment when you resolved to stay in that seat, you reclaimed your humanity and you gave us all back a piece of our own. I thank you for that. I thank you for acting without concern. I often thought about what that took, knowing the climate of the times and what could have happened to you, what it took to stay seated. You acted without concern for yourself and made life better for us all. We shall not be moved. I marvel at your will. I celebrate your strength to this day. And I am forever grateful, Sister Rosa, for your courage, your conviction. I owe you to succeed. I will not be moved.

FROM OPRAH WINFREY'S EULOGY FOR ROSA PARKS

Now write your eulogy:

_____

_____

_____

_____

_____

_____

_____

_____

_____

_____

A Second Exercise

Here is another tool to help you determine what is important. This time you will be looking at your leadership role with others.

Assume you have just been named the leader of a new team. It is your first day on the job, and you are asked what to expect from you as a leader. You respond that they may want to contact your coworkers or direct reports from your previous job. What words would you want others to use when describing you as a leader?

A GREATER CAUSE

Religious teachers from all faiths and moral philosophers from all walks of life have grounded their teaching in the belief that we are

> For success, like happiness, cannot be pursued; it must ensure, and it only does so as the unintended side-effect of one's personal dedication to a cause greater than oneself or as the by-product of one's surrender to a person other than oneself.
>
> —*Viktor Frankl*

accountable for our actions and should serve a higher purpose. Some would tell us that these moral underpinnings are out of step with today's society. Nothing could be further from the truth.

Leaders who hold to a purpose greater than self are not blown off course by the winds of change and fashion. They are confident that their moral compass is pointing in the right direction. They are grounded and anchored in timeless principles that lead to decisions based on *what's* right rather than *who's* right.

For the Boy Scout or Girl Scout, the first duty is to God and country. Our relationship to our God defines our relationship to others. Our relationship to our country defines the boundaries of our identity and loyalty. This is not an American principle. It is a universal principle that has been adopted by Scouting organizations throughout the world since 1932. It is a universal principle that should be adopted by each of us as leaders—regardless of our position in life or worldview.

CAN YOU HAVE A HIGHER PURPOSE WITHOUT GOD?

Wars have been fought. Lies have been told. People have been abused, misled, and robbed. All of these things have been done in the name of religion—maybe not your religion, but someone's. And as a result, there are those who have come to believe that religion and integrity do not mix.

There are those who act in ways that are diametrically opposed to the religious teachings they espouse. They claim integrity, honor, tolerance, respect, and trustworthiness without any apparent commitment to living those principles.

The cynics point to the fakes as an indictment and repudiation of everyone. Their caution may be justified, but to stereotype the behavior of everyone based on the bad behavior of a few is wrong in any situation.

> Men never do evil so completely and cheerfully as when they do it from a religious conviction.
>
> —*Blaise Pascal*

The existence of the false never diminishes the value of the original as long as we can distinguish between the two. If anything, fakes only make the original even more valuable and beautiful.

Zig Ziglar, writing the Foreword for the original edition of this book, cited an April 28, 1986, issue of *Fortune* magazine that stated, "91 percent of CEOs of the Fortune 500 companies are people of faith."[5] *Business Week* noted in a 1999 article that "five years ago, only one conference on spirituality and the workplace could be identified; now there are hundreds. There are more than 10,000 Bible and prayer groups in workplaces that meet regularly."[6]

Dr. Tony Campolo, professor emeritus of Sociology at Eastern University, describes the importance of being in complete balance by using the Chinese principles of *Yin* and *Yang*. Yin, according to Campolo, is being sensitive to person. Yang is being sensitive to principle.[7] Too much concern over what people think of you creates the temptation to abandon principles. Too much concern over principle can cause you to forget the impact of your decisions on people. Leaders use their faith as an opportunity to integrate and balance all aspects of their life. Our responsibility is to pay less attention to what people say about their religion and more attention to how they act in accordance with their faith.

You can aspire to a higher purpose without reference to God or religion. Some people call it nature, while others call it God. And, there are others who simply feel a presence that they are unable to explain. The truly successful people lead their lives and build their careers on a solid moral and ethical base that is exemplified through faith in someone or something greater than themselves.

True service to a cause greater than oneself causes leaders to operate from a sense of stewardship. They are as competitive as anyone, and they seek to win. They simply operate from the belief that immediate gratification is not the same as long-term success.

LEADER OR LIAR?

We make the choice every day . . . are we leaders or liars?

This is no blanket accusation of malicious or criminal behavior. Most people have good and honorable intentions, and they want to do what's right. Here is the challenge: We know our intentions, but others do not. They simply look at our behavior and performance filtered through their lens of perception. We are evaluated on a simple standard: Did we do what we said we would do?

We may see ourselves as a leader, but others may perceive that we are lying to them or ourselves.

The failure to live up to your good intentions can occur in any aspect of life. And though these failures are not intentional, the net effect is a loss of trust in your ability to honorably influence the actions and outcomes of others.

Imagine yourself wearing a large button with the words "Leader" and "Liar" written in such a way that one of the words is always readable to others. How would the people you wish to influence read the button you're wearing? Would they read Leader or Liar? Their vision is in direct proportion to their ability to follow you in good times and bad.

INTEGRITY IN A BANKRUPTCY

There are some who rationalize their behavior for the sake of expediency or gain. Honor and integrity may cost us our survival. Yet, whatever the cost, integrity-driven leaders hold true to their principles. As a result, they retain honor even in a situation that many consider dishonorable.

For instance, many passengers felt Braniff International Airways did not act honorably during its first bankruptcy in 1982. When Braniff recalled planes in flight, passengers lost the price of their tickets and were stranded, people were irate. While the corporate reputation was sullied, most of those who came under attack—agents, flight attendants, pilots, and even Braniff president Howard Putnam—acted with a great deal of integrity and desire to do what was right within the legal constraints that required them to protect the company's remaining assets—its airplanes.

Putnam was president of the then up-and-coming regional carrier Southwest Airlines when he was first contacted by Braniff's board of directors. He took the job and promised the board to do his best to rescue the troubled carrier. As soon as he took office, he found that the airline only had a 10-day cash reserve. If he stayed in his post, there was only a slight chance he could save the airline. If he left immediately, he could probably get another job and avoid a black mark on his record. Yet he had made a promise and felt a promise made was a debt unpaid. He decided to stay with Braniff, do what he could to save it, and if he couldn't, to ride the airline down along with everyone else.

In retrospect, Putnam's honesty and integrity may have contributed to the airline's demise. In the waning days of Braniff's fight to continue operations, a reporter asked Putnam if he could guarantee that Braniff would be flying in a year. Putnam, in a sense putting professional death before dishonor, stated no one could guarantee any company's success or failure. When pressed further, he stated that he felt good about the company's prospects, but could not guarantee its survival. The newspaper's report that Putnam was unsure of Braniff's survival resulted in further negative publicity.

The discipline of personal integrity is easy when times are good. The true test of our commitment to stand up for the principles and purpose in which we believe occurs when we are tempted to act in our own immediate self-interest rather than with a sense of honor and integrity. Putnam did not act in his best self-interest, but he acted with integrity.

Kenneth Goodpaster, Koch Professor of Business Ethics at the University of St. Thomas, wrote, "The corporate leader who balances economic competition, legal compliance, and moral responsibility imposes upon self and company a fuller agenda than the leader concerned only with profitability and legality."[8]

For Howard Putnam, it came down to a sense of duty—the duty to honor the legal obligations mandated in a bankruptcy proceeding and the duty to follow his core. Balancing the two wasn't easy.

Most of the passengers inconvenienced by Braniff's decision to bring all the planes to a central location for protection were offered free transportation home by other carriers. Braniff was unable to provide assistance. Braniff was allowed to keep 250 of its 10,000 employees to maintain airplanes and reorganize the company. The company was legally required to terminate everyone else at midnight on the day of the bankruptcy announcement. There was no one to answer the phones.

Putnam says, "Our number 1 responsibility was to the estate of Braniff (secured lenders, bondholders). Although it broke our hearts, that was the priority by law. Employees, public stockholders, unsecured creditors are considered lower 'classes' of stakeholders under the law."

Nevertheless, Putnam's leadership left a lasting mark on Braniff employees. Unlike most turnaround assignments taken by leaders today, Putnam did not have a golden parachute severance package as a hedge against the company's failure nor did he receive stock options for a successful turnaround. That fact created a sense of trust that was necessary to pull everyone together to save the company.

Early in his tenure at Braniff, Putnam wrote a personal letter to all 10,000 company employees. The letter explained his belief that Braniff was a great airline that deserved to fly and asked for every employee to help by sharing ideas for improvement and change. He was told to expect no more than 500 responses from 10,000 employees, so Putnam added a postscript to the letter stating that anyone who took the time to write would receive a personal, signed reply expressing his thoughts about their suggestion. The only stipulation placed on the request was that the employee had to sign his or her name.

More than 3,000 employees wrote to Putnam over three weeks, and true to his word, he personally responded to every letter. In case you are wondering, it took four months to complete the responses. Putnam wrote notes in the office, at home, in the car, and even in the men's room.[9] Former employees carried handwritten notes received from Putnam years afterward. Integrity, duty, and honor may have their costs in the short term, but they reap incredible rewards over the long haul.

In the end, Putnam's integrity won out. Braniff entered and exited bankruptcy in 16 months without a single shareholder suit. Putnam's handling of the restructuring became a case study at Harvard Business School.

FOLLOW YOUR CORE

Life in today's world is often a series of trade-offs and decision-making dilemmas. At the heart of every difficult decision is the question of short-term results versus long-term reputation. *Following your core* means making better choices when faced with the temptation to do otherwise.

In organizations, leaders are presented with choices that affect the lives and safety of customers, employees, and suppliers. In our personal lives, choices affect the security, cohesiveness, and survival of our families. In our communities, leaders make decisions that have an impact for generations to come.

ETHICS LITMUS TEST

Many years ago, Dr. Harry Emerson Fosdick created a six-point test for deciding right from wrong[10] that was later adapted by Dr. Preston Bradley. We revised and honed it into the Ethics Litmus Test: Six questions to ask yourself in any questionable or difficult situation. A positive answer to each lets you know you are following the core values and acting with personal integrity. Take the test:

1. Is the course of action you plan to follow logical, responsible, and legal?

2. Would the results be beneficial for all if everyone made the same decision?

3. Where will your plan of action lead? How will it affect others?

4. Will you think well of yourself when you look back at what you've done?

5. How would the person you most admire handle this situation? What would that person do?

6. What would your family and friends think of your decision? Decisions made in the hope that no one will find out are usually wrong.

INTEGRITY FOR A MARKET OF ONE

The story of Raymond Dunn and Gerber Baby Foods is perhaps the most compelling example I've found of an organization that followed its core and turned intention into action. What would you do to follow your core? Would you retool your plant to manufacture a free product? Would your employees volunteer their time to manufacture it? Even if it was for a market of one?

This amazing story came to my attention in July 1990:

Raymond Dunn, Jr., turned 16 Tuesday in Yankee Lake, Sullivan County, New York, but the profoundly retarded birthday boy feasted not on cake, to which he is allergic, but on the day's greatest gift: the bland, brown infant formula that keeps him alive.

Gerber Products Co., which stopped making the meat-based formula in 1985, resumed production two months ago after Raymond's doctors said that he would die without it. Gerber employees volunteered to make a batch on their own time, and on June 26 the Dunns received a two-year supply free of charge.[11]

"By 1988, Carol Dunn had hunted down every can she could find, and Gerber had exhausted its backlog. The mother begged Gerber to make more."[12] *Along the way, the company remained in contact with the Dunn family, providing its remaining stock for free and notifying the family about any new formula that Raymond might be able to tolerate.*[13]

The company agreed to manufacture the product for a market of one in 1990. "Research division volunteers put their own projects on hold, hauled out old equipment and devoted several thousand square feet and several days of production time and space to Raymond's MBF. They even had to go to Washington to get USDA approval for the label."[14]

Reflecting on the company's generosity, Raymond's mother Carol said, "Gerber says, 'Babies are our business,' but Raymond is their business, too."[15]

AND NOW FOR THE REST OF THE STORY

Gerber's commitment to service was not a one-time publicity ploy. The Dunn's had a one-year supply of food remaining when Raymond died in January 1995 at the age of 20. The company produced and shipped the product at no expense for years after the initial story captured the hearts of people everywhere. That's quite a commitment for a market of one.

Raymond's life prompted compassion and caring from people everywhere. Volunteers made themselves available to constantly be with him, feed him, and brush his teeth after each meal. Many were motivated by the newspaper stories of Gerber's generosity. SullivanArc, a not-for-profit organization that serves the developmentally disabled in Sullivan County, New York, even named a home in Raymond's honor in 1999.[16]

What would you do to live your values and the values of your organization? That question must be answered every day. Gerber didn't make money by helping Raymond. In fact, it cost them money. The story of Raymond Dunn and Gerber proves that a commitment to integrity pays emotional and reputation dividends that reach further than immediate financial returns.

HOW ABOUT YOUR LIFE?

Longfellow's sentiments are inspiring, but few people will leave footprints on the sands of time that more than a handful will ever notice.

> Lives of great men all remind us; We too can make our lives sublime; And departing, leave behind us; Footprints on the sands of time.
>
> —*Henry Wadsworth Longfellow*

Sure. Who wouldn't want to have their name associated with the great leaders of the world, or at least in their profession? That is a noble aspiration even if it were only for the 15 minutes of fame that Andy Warhol is reputed to have promised.

We often associate greatness with fame. We glamorize others' actions and assign them hero status. There's nothing wrong with heroes. We need more of them as role models in our world. But fame is not success.

It is often luck—the special circumstances that arise when, as legendary football coach Vince Lombardi said, "preparation meets opportunity."

Viktor Frankl had years to contemplate the meaning of life in the harshest of conditions. He believed that "Life ultimately means taking the responsibility to find the right answer to its problems and to fulfill the tasks which it constantly sets for the individual."[17]

We may never be counted among the world's best, but we should always be counted on to *do our best*. To do the work of living in the most positive manner possible is the ultimate example for others. The few we influence today have the potential to influence the multitudes tomorrow. As we said in Chapter 2, there are always eyes watching us.

A CODE TO LIVE BY

If you are looking for a set of principles by which to lead a life that is known for its personal integrity, there is no better list than the 12 principles articulated in the Scout Law:

A Scout is

1. **Trustworthy.** Trust is the basis for all successful relationships and the most important task of leadership in changing times. Without trust, people do not feel free to look at options for mutual success, and believability diminishes. You can count on trustworthy leaders to focus on what's right rather than who's right, to be consistent in their dealings with people, and to be honest.

2. **Loyal.** The loyal leader has the courage to stand by and stand up for others. She looks for creative ways to help those she leads meet their goals. She doesn't throw others "under the bus" rather than accepting responsibility for her own performance.

> You can get everything in life you want if you'll help enough other people get what they want.
>
> —*Zig Ziglar*

3. **Helpful.** Being helpful pays dividends—internally and externally. The internal dividend comes in the good feeling you get when you realize that you have assisted someone in reaching a goal or solving a problem. The external dividend comes from the reciprocity you receive when you help others.

4. **Friendly.** Leaders may be given the right to lead, but they earn the right to be followed. Being friendly communicates a humanness that commands respect. Friendliness doesn't have to mean being best friends. It does mean acknowledging people as individuals with their own special personalities and likes.

5. **Courteous.** The root of courtesy is respect. The leader with integrity respects the opinions, beliefs, customs, and values of others. He encourages individuals to state their opinions and then listens. He respects beliefs and values and doesn't impose his own morals on others, choosing instead to let his behavior speak for him. The leader who practices courtesy does these things and more, continually looking for ways to make the people around him feel important.

6. **Kind.** Integrity-driven leaders have a high level of self-esteem. They have no need to make others look bad in order to make themselves look better. They demonstrate their self-esteem through kindness. Kindness is not the same as being unwilling to say something bad to someone. Kindness means that we design an approach that enables people to preserve their dignity and helps them improve.

7. **Obedient.** Obedience to the rules can be viewed as opposite of what it takes to succeed in today's business environment. The obedience of which we speak is positive, however. Obedience in this context brings to mind words such as *loyal, faithful, devoted,*

conforming, and *law abiding.* The individual who leads with integrity is obedient to the rules of the organization, his or her own code of honor, and the natural laws that govern how the world works.

8. **Cheerful.** The book of Proverbs says, effectively, "A cheerful heart is good medicine."[18] This medicine works for you and all those around you. Scientific evidence points to the fact that the individual who is cheerful experiences less stress and has better health than those who continually worry. Common sense and experience tell us that, all things being equal, people prefer to be around other people who have a cheerful outlook.

9. **Thrifty.** Leaders understand that success is based on what they keep, not what they make. Thrifty leaders are willing to spend money, to achieve a goal, but as former client Roy Christensen of the Black Mountain Spring Water Company says, "We try to make our dimes work like dollars."

10. **Brave.** Historically, bravery is thought of in the physical sense. Today, bravery most often applies to the courage to follow your dreams and convictions. It is tempting to sacrifice aspirations and principles on the altar of expediency. Sticking to your goal and your principles is just as scary as physical dangers.

11. **Clean.** A former tennis coach had a saying that describes the importance of a clean body, mind, and spirit. "If you look sharp, you feel sharp. If you feel sharp, you act sharp. If you act sharp, you play sharp. If you play sharp, you are sharp."

12. **Reverent.** Reverence is a word related to "awe." We should never lose our awe for our creator, for creation, or for human potential. Individuals who respect themselves and command the respect of others have a sense of reverence that runs deep and still like a mighty river.

WHAT WILL YOU DO?

A few honest mistakes do not brand us as terminal liars. Even the best leader has an occasional bad day. Remember, it is the rare journey that unfolds without a single setback. Becoming an integrity-driven leader is a continuous challenge to be better today than you were yesterday.

Intention without action is a lie. Commit to a course of action. Do just one thing different today, and then build on that success.

Spend quiet time at the beginning of each day reviewing your commitments and preplaying your actions as an integrity-driven leader. Spend a few moments at the end of each day replaying your shortcomings as a success.

There is great power in the discipline of personal integrity. It enables us to be authentic rather than submit to others' preconceived notions. It empowers us to live positively and handle temptations and challenges, and it encourages us to set an example that, in our own way, leaves footprints on the sands of time.

CHAPTER FOUR

MASTER THE ART OF
INTERPERSONAL INTEGRITY

When you deal with the souls of men, take off your
shoes. You walk on sacred ground.

—BLAINE LEE, PH.D.

JOSE NIÑO KNOWS ABOUT leading diverse groups. As the president of the U.S. Hispanic Chamber of Commerce for eight years, Niño saw the number of Hispanic Chambers of Commerce increase from 30 to 258. Hispanic-owned businesses in the United States grew from 250,000 to 1,300,000. Those results are even more impressive when you look past the traditional assumptions that can oversimplify his accomplishment.

During our conversation, Niño said, "As Latino leaders, we've had to lead in Spanish, and we've had to lead in English. We have to live and lead while being cognizant of bridging two different worlds to move forward.

"You can't assume that everyone automatically shares the same goals and interests. The Mexican Americans from Texas have a different agenda from the Mexican Americans from Southern California. The Mexican Americans from Southern California have a different agenda from the

Mexican Americans in Northern California. The same could be said of the relationships between any of the national groups represented in what many with little familiarity with the region would assume to be a cohesive group: Central Americans, South Americans, Cubans, Puerto Ricans, and Spaniards all come from different perspectives. Two Central American countries—El Salvador and Honduras—went to war due to a previous disagreement and an altercation after an international soccer match. There have been disagreements over economic issues, and there are many different agendas. They didn't necessarily want to work together."

Niño's experience is a valuable lesson for all of us. Departments and teams in your workplace don't necessarily have the same goals or want to work together just because the paychecks come from the same place. Neighborhoods are often at odds despite being in the same town or city. Similar examples exist in the places in which we worship, learn, purchase our goods and services, and socialize.

Influencing others through interpersonal relationships is an essential part of any leader's job. Doing this while maintaining your integrity is an art that is only perfected over time. To help you, there are skills you can develop and knowledge you can acquire. The art of leadership is knowing when to use the correct skill or piece of knowledge. Niño's success is a model for leadership worth emulating. It can be traced to five essential principles:

1. Be authentic and transparent.

2. Establish power based on trust.

3. Stay flexible without being loose.

4. Honor others.

5. Practice the FFP Factor.

The information in this chapter will provide ideas and strategies you can use to become a master of interpersonal integrity.

THREE WAYS TO INFLUENCE OTHERS

Would you rather see integrity, hear integrity, or feel integrity? This is not a trick question. If we are to believe Emerson, actions trump words in demonstrating our integrity. And yet, there are many situations where the only way we experience a leader's integrity is through the words he or she speaks and the way those words make us feel.

> **What you are speaks so loudly, I cannot hear what you say.**
>
> *—Ralph Waldo Emerson*

Take, for instance, any national election. There are those who believe every promise of their chosen candidate—regardless of the candidate's ability to actually deliver on that promise—because of the manner in which the message was delivered or the feelings the candidate was able to inspire. We usually have no way of judging whether that candidate can actually accomplish all that is promised, but we vote according to what we believe his or her *intentions* are and because we believe that candidate has the skills to actuate those intentions.

The candidate's supporters believe that every disparaging remark about their chosen candidate is a complete fabrication while every unfounded rumor about the opposing candidate is the absolute truth. But we live in a world where truth is elusive. In fact, there are undoubtedly truths to both sides.

The 2008 U.S. presidential election provides an amazing example of this. Each candidate's supporters believed the best of their own nominee and the worst of their opponent. Both John McCain and Barack Obama put forth ideas that were simultaneously embraced and ridiculed depending on your point of view. McCain's detractors evaluated his long history of integrity and service against distrust of his party's leadership over the previous eight years. Obama's history of service to country was, by function of his age, shorter. His ideas for change were evaluated by his detractors against distrust of the message and the perceived inexperience of the messenger.

Much has been and will be written about why Obama won this election. Some point to the historic aspects of being the United States' first African-American candidate or the discipline of his campaign. Others mention a host of factors that went wrong in the McCain campaign, backlash against the outgoing administration or the bad timing of the economic meltdown of 2008. In the end, this election was won the way that all elections are won . . . or lost. Voters volunteer their support for the candidate that they believe will provide the best solutions to the challenges they face. Obama's ability to create a relationship with voters and communicate his intentions moved a majority of the voters to trust him, and that made all the difference.

Such is the nature of influence in today's world. And it is a phenomenon that is not limited to political races. Corporate leaders, supervisors, managers, parents, teachers, and clergy all rely on the words they speak and the relationships they foster to influence others.

So . . . would you rather see integrity, hear integrity, or feel integrity? Emerson was correct that actions speak louder than words, but in today's world words and relationships often precede action as the vehicle for influencing others. Interpersonal integrity—the ability to relate to others in an authentic manner that builds trust—is a crucial skill. The integrity-driven leader understands that there are three factors that influence interpersonal relationships with others:

1. **Being:** Who we are speaks louder than our words once others have the opportunity to see us in action.

2. **Telling:** The messages we use to let people know where we stand and what we believe.

3. **Relating:** The connection we make with others. Being and telling contribute to relating, but the masters at building strong relationships have the ability to form a connection that goes beyond their words and actions. They make us feel as if they understand, accept, and appreciate us.

Congruence and consistency between these three factors are the hallmarks of an integrity-driven leader. We want to see, hear, and feel integrity. Blaine Lee, writing in *The Power Principle* put it beautifully: "When you match your words, feelings, thoughts, and actions with congruence and without duplicity, you are exercising integrity."[1]

WHAT HAPPENS WHEN INTERPERSONAL INTEGRITY EXISTS

Integrity and honor in our interpersonal relationships transform our lives. They create a true sense of partnership and remove the friction that is created when mistrust is evident.

Interpersonal integrity also alters the manner in which we deal with others. You explain the why rather than dictate the what. No one feels the need to be anything other than who they are. The foundation of trust that had been created allows candor and honesty to freely flow in the relationship. There is authenticity and alignment.

WHY GANDHI STILL INSPIRES US

During seminars and workshops, I often ask participants to list and share the names of leaders who model the principles of integrity-driven leadership. Mahatma Gandhi's name regularly appears in these lists as an example of consistency and alignment between thought, word, and deed that had a profound and lasting influence on countless lives. Gandhi's crusade for civil rights and independence for his country through nonviolent social protest became the example for similar struggles throughout the world.

Gandhi had total alignment between the being, telling, and relating aspects of his life. And as a result, his ability to relate to people through honor and integrity gave him immense power to influence everyone with whom he came in to contact—even his adversaries.

At one point, the British government invited Gandhi to attend the Round Table Conference and speak to the House of Commons in England. Gandhi appeared not as the impressive leader those in attendance expected but as a small man in simple robes. He spoke not as a charismatic orator but as a soft-spoken man with an abundant heart and clear mission.

Gandhi spoke for nearly two hours without notes. Some people in the audience were genuinely moved and began to relate to both the man and his cause. At the end of his presentation, many of those who had sanctioned Gandhi's imprisonment and passed laws to suppress the Indian people's right for independence rushed to the front of the room to speak to him.

The press wondered how his adversaries could be so moved to embrace this quiet leader. And in the process of questioning Mahadev Desai, Gandhi's secretary, someone asked about his ability to speak for hours without notes.

Desai's response to their question about Gandhi's ability must have taken them by surprise. He said:

> *You don't understand Gandhi. You see, what he thinks is what he feels. What he feels is what he says. And what he says is what he does. What Gandhi thinks, what he feels, what he says, and what he does are all the same. He does not need notes. You and I think things, which sometimes may be different than what we feel. What we say depends on who is listening. What we do depends on who is watching. It is not so with him. He needs no notes.*[2]

Gandhi's alignment between feelings and thought, words, and action is the authenticity and transparency of which Jose Niño speaks. It cements your reputation with your allies and establishes credibility with those who do not necessarily agree with you. These relationships are built on integrity . . . and honor.

THE HONOR PRINCIPLE

The word *honor* is traditionally associated with either one's character or with being held in high regard. There is another definition of the word honor, however—to treat with great respect and importance. This interpretation implies performance in pursuit of a goal.

Taken together, we have the Honor Principle: *The honors of long-term success follow the consistent honoring of others through integrity and personal performance.* Applied to the important task of building relationships, it means that the trust, loyalty, and commitment we desire are the result of going beyond minimum expectations to truly honor others.

> **What is left when honor is lost?**
>
> —*Publilius Syrus*

The Honor Principle is realized when we consistently apply three concepts: alignment, admiration, and assurance:

- **Alignment enables individuals to be their best and focus their efforts toward achieving goals honorably.** Alignment between words and actions builds trusting relationships and personal credibility. Values aligned with universal principles provide a foundation for making good and honorable decisions. Alignment between actions and priorities creates a sense of urgency and generates energy to sustain efforts.

- **Admiration is defined as a feeling of wonder, pleasure, or approval.**[3] Admiration changes the way you approach even your staunchest critic. It reframes the conversation, and it forces you to look at possibilities for cooperation rather than barriers to achieving the desired goal. Admiring others and ourselves means we build on positive attributes and create the expectation for success. Admiration leads us to give the best we have to offer out of personal desire rather than mandated compliance.

- **Assurance provides the guarantee of both word and deed.** True assurance comes from a deep sense of accountability and a personal commitment to doing whatever it takes to honor promises, priorities, and purpose. In business, assurance is reflected through the commitment to quality in products, services, and relationships. In personal relationships, it is the follow-through on a promise. The dedication to assurance drives us to perfect our performance and do whatever it takes to correct mistakes when they occur.

The audience members who were moved by Gandhi's quiet and confident arguments about why the nation of India should be independent experienced the Honor Principle in action.

Gandhi's alignment was previously addressed. Admiration and assurance were also present even in the face of disagreement. Admiration doesn't necessarily require agreement. It certainly doesn't allow you to withhold the truth or tell people only what they want to hear. The admiration defined by the Honor Principle requires us to look at the best possibilities in each situation.

Likewise, Gandhi's audience knew of his assurance before he ever entered the room. They had experienced the consistency of his actions. They had seen the congruency of his beliefs through his actions. And, it was on display in the presentation. Imagine the disconnect if the individual teaching nonviolent civil disobedience had engaged in shouting, shoving, or other aggressive acts.

BUT, I'M NOT GANDHI

I know. Neither am I. As I wrote this section about alignment, admiration, and assurance, I found myself thinking about all the areas in which I fall short. There are times when I have said what I thought others wanted to hear rather than what needed to be said. There are times when I have dealt with people from a position of dislike and disdain rather than admiration. There are even people with whom the closest I will come to admiration is acceptance.

I wondered if Gandhi ever knew how he influenced the world. Surely this leader who oozed integrity from every pore of his being realized how heroic he was. Here is what he said:

> *I claim to be no more than an average man with less than average ability. I am not a visionary. I claim to be a practical idealist. Nor can I claim any special merit for what I have been able to achieve with laborious research. I have not the shadow of a doubt that any man or woman can achieve what I have, if he or she would make the same effort and cultivate the same hope and faith.*[4]

The leader you want to be is inside you just waiting to be released. It's definitely not easy, and it certainly takes a great deal of work. I may never make it but I know I surely won't if I do not try. How about you?

I suspect that if we could ask Gandhi for his advice he would say that doing nothing is the one sure way to *never* reach the level of honor and integrity to which we aspire.

> **The most serious mistakes are not being made as a result of wrong answers. The truly dangerous thing is asking the wrong questions.**
>
> —*Peter Drucker*

THREE QUESTIONS TO ANSWER NOW

Time management techniques have long emphasized the importance of doing first things first. Building interpersonal relationships based on the Honor Principle requires going beyond traditional time management. It is not enough to do first things first. You must also do first things well.

The following questions provide direction as you put the Honor Principle into practice:

1. **What areas of my performance are not aligned?** Where are the gaps between the promises made and daily practice? For your organization, where are areas where policies, practices, and procedures are not consistent with mission, vision, values, and brand statements? For your personal and family relationships, where are your actions out of sync with the promises you made and the principles in which you profess to believe?

2. **What can I legitimately and ethically do to show my admiration?** Where are the opportunities to show my true appreciation and admiration for others with whom I come in contact? How can I express a sense of hope and admiration for the people with whom I disagree?

3. **How can I assure the quality of my performance and relationships?** What are the strengths on which I can build? Where are the opportunities to improve processes and systems so that assurances occur by design rather than by accident?

THREE TYPES OF POWER

You have three types of power at your disposal as a leader: fear, utility, and trust.

Fear

Leaders who wield power through fear create environments where others are intimidated. Their response to every interpersonal relationship is to overwhelm the other person with force. Perhaps you have seen or experienced leaders who relate to others through fear. We're not talking about being straightforward, having high expectations, or even being gruff. The leader who derives his power through fear belittles and threatens. In less obvious cases, deception and trickery are used to exert control.

> **Don't be afraid to take a big step when one is indicated. You can't cross a chasm in two small steps.**
>
> *—David Lloyd George*

There are times when fear, compliance, and force appear to be the appropriate strategy for getting others to do what you want. Fear is quick, easy, and to the point. You don't have to take time to explain.

And, fear works . . . in the short run. People will do what you want them to do to avoid immediate pain. But, fear and the threats that go along with them rarely work to build personal responsibility. You can mandate compliance, but commitment is volunteered. And, who wants to volunteer to be intimidated?

Individuals who are led solely by fear and intimidation eventually learn to get by, get out, or get even. Often, the threat of punishment created by fear-based power does very little to change behavior or performance. People simply learn not to get caught. Think of your own experience as a teenager. When you were caught and punished for sneaking out of the house at night to hang out with your friends, did you stop the behavior? Or, did you just get better at it?

Utility

We have all experienced utility-based power. I give you a day's work, and you give me a day's pay. I clean my room, and you allow me to go to the mall. I remember your birthday, and you remember mine.

The principles of reciprocity and fairness govern utility-based power. They are the foundation on which day-to-day transactions are built. And, their origin dates back to the earliest days of human interaction. Archeologist

Richard Leakey said, "We are human because our ancestors learned to share their food and their skills in an honored network of obligation."[5]

Robert Cialdini shares this story in his classic book, *Influence: How and Why People Agree to Things*:

> *A university professor sent cards to a sample of perfect strangers. Although he expected some reaction, the response he received was amazing—holiday cards addressed to him came pouring back from the people who had never met nor heard of him. The great majority of those who returned a card never inquired into the identity of the unknown professor.*[6]

This study—though small—represents the power of the reciprocity and utility as a way to influence. Utility-based power is logical, reasonable, and relatively efficient. The best transactional relationships are also fair, honest, and open. Everyone gets what they want and is pleased with the results. What's not to like?

There is nothing necessarily wrong or dishonest about utility-based power. It works well for many or even most of the relationships we experience in life. Business, contracts, and commerce are historically based on this quid pro quo approach to getting things done.

The problem with utility-based power comes when we have nothing left to offer that the other person values. At work, we lose star employees because we can't match the value offered by a competitor. At home, relationships fall apart when one person comes to feel that staying with the other is no longer worth it because there is a "better offer."

A second problem with utility-based power is what happens when the perception of fairness has been broken. Here's an example:

> *Martha found a new job with more challenge in a better environment. That was the story she told her manager, and she was sticking to it . . . until . . .*

> *In reality, Martha was miserable. Her boss led through fear*
> *and intimidation. She had been asked illegal questions about her*
> *plans to have a baby when she accepted the job, and inappropriate*
> *jokes and comments were the standard rather than the exception.*
> *She lived with it as long as should could because she needed the job.*
> *Martha gave the 30-day notice that was expected for her profes-*
> *sional role. Her manager responded by terminating her immedi-*
> *ately. And that is where reciprocity deteriorated into the desire for*
> *revenge.*
> *"It was bad enough that the manager was a jerk, but I was*
> *willing to do the right thing," Martha said. "But now he's not even*
> *going to honor my resignation notice?"*
> *When Martha threatened legal action based on the history of*
> *inappropriate comments, the company paid a 30-day severance*
> *and received no work in return. All of this happened because a*
> *leader decided to break the perception of fairness that is the foun-*
> *dation for all reciprocal agreements.*

And that's the danger. Utility-based power and the reciprocity it requires can be used for good to serve the highest needs, or it can be used as an instrument of manipulation. It must be protected with integrity at all costs.

Robert Dilenschneider has advised and counseled leaders and leading organizations throughout the world. He cautions, "The temptation and the means (especially in our age of highly sophisticated electronic communications) often exist to do the expedient, the immoral, or even the illegal for the sake of the greater goal. My advice is simple: Don't."[7]

Trust

There is a level of interpersonal relationships beyond the reciprocal, utility-based transactions that exist in our lives and organizations. It is the power of trust.

The dictionary defines trust as "reliance on the integrity, strength, ability, or surety of a person or thing."[8] At a core level, trust is necessary for transactional, utility-based power to exist. Jose Niño says, "we trust each other so much that we trust others will stop at stop signs."

Relationships built on trust have the power to move us past the transactional and become transformative. Trust is the lubricant that removes friction from relationships. It gives people confidence to embrace change. It empowers people to say what's on their minds. Trust is the ultimate power to influence others to cooperate and act in ways that, on the surface, appear to not be in their immediate self-interest.

Trust doesn't require explanation or question motives. There is a history of honorable intention and integrity. Trust is the result of being trustworthy. It is as simple and as complex as that.

HOW LEADERS BECOME TRUSTWORTHY

Five factors that contribute to a leader's ability to earn and maintain trust are:

1. **Character:** Are you honest? No one wants to feel as if they are being lied to. People want to be told the truth even if it is bad news. This is critical regardless of your line of work. Even the Mafia wants honest people working for them.

2. **Competence:** Are you capable? The willing leader who does not develop the capacity to earn the trust of others is just as ineffective as the skilled leader who is unwilling to use those talents for the greater good.

3. **Consistency:** Are you reliable? There is a two-word moniker for inconsistent leaders who don't follow through and change on a whim. It is not a nice word. Trust me—you don't want to be known for this.

4. **Communication:** Do you share information openly, seek to understand others' views, and provide a forum for disagreement? The best leaders share information openly, honestly, and to the extent possible, freely.

5. **Courage:** Are you willing to do what's right even when it is not convenient? There will be a time when you will be called on to take action or make a decision that shows the world you can be counted on in any situation. This will not be pleasant, but it will define your leadership legacy.

THE FFP FACTOR

James Patterson and Peter Kim wrote a book titled *The Day America Told the Truth.* I still find it fascinating even after many reads. These gentlemen received responses from over 2,000 people in 50 locations across the United States during a one-week period. One of the results was a listing of 72 occupations ranked on the basis of the respondents belief in their honesty and integrity.

You may find it interesting to know that the president of the United States came in at number 35, just behind construction workers and plumbers. Congressmen came in at number 66—behind rock stars and car salesmen but ahead of local politicians.[9]

Three occupations comprise the FFP Factor named in honor of the first letters in those occupations: Firefighter, Farmer, and Paramedic.

So what makes us look to firefighters, farmers, and paramedics as examples of honor and integrity? And more important, what does that have to do with interpersonal relationships?

Firefighters, farmers, and paramedics relate to us at a core level of sustenance and security. But that alone is not enough to deserve our trust.

The answer is service. Most would agree that the individuals who commit to these professions are not in it for the money. And there are probably firefighters, farmers, and paramedics who do not perform their

> **The only authority deserving one's allegiance is that which is freely and knowingly granted by the led to the leader, in response to, and in proportion to, the clearly evident servant stature of the leader. Those who choose to follow this principle will not casually accept the authority of existing institutions. Rather, they will freely respond only to individuals who are chosen as leaders because they are proven and trusted as servants.[10]**
>
> —*Robert K. Greenleaf*

jobs with the most noble of intentions. Yet the best of the best in these professions—the ones we picture in our minds when asked to rank professions on the basis of honesty and integrity—approach their jobs every day from a sense of service.

Leadership is a relationship that is earned. Management is a position that is granted. Trust as a leader is in direct proportion to your ability to serve the highest needs of followers. Nowhere is that more evident than in the area of communication.

LEADING WITH RELATIONSHIPS

Carl Sewell has built one of the leading automobile dealerships in America by continuously and conscientiously applying two simple principles—turn one-time buyers into lifetime customers and be the best at what you do. It is a philosophy based on the value of relationships.

Customers *see* the external symbols of the Sewell philosophy: free loan cars, extended service hours, and immaculate facilities. They *experience* and *feel* a sincere desire to deliver a level of service that can best be described by a single word: exceptional.

Sewell remembers the specific incident that led to his decision to build an organization that distinguishes itself: He was a young man working in his father's car dealership, and the business experienced three instances of poor customer service in the same day. The experience affected him deeply. He did not want to live like that, and he did not want to have a reputation for running a business like that. Serendipitously, an associate meeting was to be held the next day. Young Sewell stood up before the staff and made the commitment to helping the company and the people in it become the best.

Extending yourself for the customer is expected at the Sewell Automotive Companies. So is extending yourself for your fellow associates. There are leaders at every turn, and their willingness to help others is a primary reason for everyone's individual and collective success. Sewell believes, "You have a responsibility as an associate to reach out to fellow associates and help them when they are not feeling good or when they are not having a great day because one day that will be you. And, you hope that someone will reach out to you."

This level of dedication to excellence and commitment to relationships is not an accident. Sewell told me, "I don't think you can be in this company very long—maybe a week without getting the feeling that exceptional performance is really the standard."[11]

The company looks for dedication to the principles of relationships, integrity, and performance in the new associates it hires. It continuously reinforces those messages through communication, rewards, and accountability. Most important, leaders at every level—beginning with Carl Sewell—model those principles every day.

Carl Sewell is quick to acknowledge that neither he nor his company is perfect. That provides motivation for improvement each day. He is also convinced that the success of his business is directly connected to the quality of the people who work there. It is a belief that is anchored not in the success of the leader, but the success of the team. It starts and ends with relationships, integrity, and performance.

TRUST AND COMMUNICATION

The Trust Factors @ Work Study, completed in early 2004, showed that communication issues are critical to employee trust. In fact, over 30 percent of the more than 1,000 thematic responses we analyzed dealt specifically with communication. Two behaviors, communicating openly and providing the needed amount of availability or communication, accounted for over 22 percent of all responses. Listening and communicating in a demeaning style were also cited as important communication behaviors.[12]

Leadership requires effective communication. The message from the employees participating in this survey is clear: Employees trust leaders who communicate. Doing so conveys a sense of service rather than an air of superiority. It provides people with what they need to succeed, and it creates an environment where people are free to respond with their commitment and support.

TRUST IN ACTION: MARY KAY ASH

Mary Kay Ash founded Mary Kay Cosmetics in 1963, and since that time, it has grown to become a multibillion-dollar global cosmetics company with more than 3,600 corporate employees and 1.8 million beauty consultants in over thirty countries.

I had the honor of interviewing Ash in 1990, eleven years before her death on Thanksgiving Day in 2001. At the time of our conversation, she was still actively involved in the company. I am often asked what it was like to spend time with Ash. My response is always the same: As cool as you think it might be to spend 45 minutes with this legendary woman, it was better. Here is what she told me:

I had opinions about the organizations I'd worked for. There had been many things I thought should have been done another way . . . I decided to write my memoirs—actually, a book that would help other women overcome some of the obstacles I had encountered. First, I wrote down all the good things the companies I had been with had done and then the changes I would make to create

> *a company that was based on the Golden Rule. Wouldn't it be marvelous, I kept thinking, if someone would actually start such a company? And then I realized that I didn't have to sit and wish—I could start that dream company because I had already discovered the ideal product . . . To me, "P" and "L" meant more than profit and loss—it meant people and love.*[13]

People and love are descriptive words for Mary Kay Cosmetics. Ash didn't just talk about loving people—she lived it. That's what made her one of the most respected businesspeople in history. The love began with her sales force and employees, and it extended to her customers.

Here's How It Happens

The Mary Kay company is a reflection of Mary Kay Ash, the person. It is impossible to separate the values of the organization from those of its founder. Ash believed in a set of priorities that placed God first, family second, and career third. She believed the Golden Rule should be the way everyone is treated every day and in every situation. She believed in the pursuit of the greater good and making everyone feel important. She knew that everything was subject to change except your principles. Ash's leadership style was heavy on enthusiastic encouragement and praise.

> The final test of a leader is that he leaves behind him in other men the conviction and the will to carry on.
>
> —*Walter Lippman*

The Mary Kay company is legendary for its commitment to living these values. The company doesn't promote a specific philosophy of religion or spirituality. It does promote balance, teamwork, and treating everyone with respect. The work environment is engaging, rewarding, and promotes a feeling of family. The company also has a rich history of social responsibility with causes that were near to its founder's heart.

Then there is the encouragement and praise. Mary Kay Cosmetics gives pink Cadillacs to top performers. But then, many sales organizations reward their stars with incentives. The true example of Ash's commitment to encouragement and praise is what happens before someone has earned the coveted pink Cadillac.

Training for the new sales consultant focuses on what went right—not what went wrong—no matter how many mistakes are made. Each consultant receives a ribbon for her first $100 show, another for her first $200 show, and so on. Milestones are marked with diamond rings and trips abroad. At awards ceremonies, as many people as possible are publicly rewarded and praised. They honor initial and entry-level achievements all the way up to the crowning of the queens, complete with satin sashes, tiaras, a bouquet of long-stemmed roses (pink, of course), and prizes like diamond rings, mink coats—and the crown jewels—diamond bumblebees! Why bumblebees? Because it is aerodynamically impossible for the bumblebee to fly because of its weight and wing configuration—but the bumblebee doesn't know it and flies anyway!

With this much enthusiasm, some are initially skeptical. Many people find it hard to believe that the Mary Kay company is for real, but it is. In a world filled with hyperbole and sales hype, it's easy to become somewhat jaundiced about a company's claims to care. Executives at Mary Kay know that, and they are patient. They know that the integrity of their actions and relationships will eventually win the skeptical over. Ash put it simply, "When you walk your talk, people know it and respond positively."

HOW YOU CAN INFLUENCE OTHERS WITH INTEGRITY

Jose Niño, Mahatma Gandhi, Carl Sewell, and Mary Kay Ash share seven similarities in the way they approach interpersonal relationships. If you are looking for specific competencies and habits to develop, start here:

1. Encourage cooperation, not competition.

2. Help others succeed.

3. Listen.

4. Explain the "why's" not just the "what's."

5. Value differences.

6. Be open, honest, and transparent in your communication.

7. Make other people feel important.

IT TAKES TIME

Good relationships, like good buildings, take time to construct and must be built brick by brick. Public relations can give your external image a boost, but you can't build a relationship with public relations alone. You don't create relationships with your spouse, significant other, or even your best friend overnight. What makes you think it is any different for others with whom you come in contact?

In the Declaration of Independence, the founders of the United States wrote, "We hold these truths to be self-evident, that all men are created equal." If we really believe that, then we'll treat all people as equals. This doesn't mean that the janitor in the building makes as much money as the president of the company, but it does mean that we treat the janitor with as much dignity, authenticity, and respect. That is the essence of honoring the laws of being helpful, friendly, courteous, and kind.

CAN IT WORK FOR ME?

JoAnn Dunham is just like most people—and then again—she isn't. Like most people, JoAnn grew up, went to school, and got a job to pay off her student loan. She started in an entry-level position, and she worked hard. She has never founded a company like Mary Kay Ash, or become a successful CEO like Carl Sewell, or led a national organization like Jose Niño. She has yet to influence the world like Gandhi.

So what makes Dunham worth writing about? She decided at an early age to lead. It is a choice that has influenced her life at every turn from when she was a 17-year-old high school student spending the summer in Africa sponsored by the American Institute of Foreign Studies to today when she is a divisional vice president for Mohawk Industries.

JoAnn rose from frontline sales and manufacturing jobs to a senior executive role in a traditionally male-dominated industry. That takes toughness and talent. And it takes integrity to do it in the right way.

I asked Dunham about the challenges of being a woman in a leadership position. She quickly noted that the Mohawk leadership goes out of its way to make decisions based on what you produce and not your race, gender, or any other physical factor. And then she acknowledged that even with that kind of support there are challenges for women in leadership.

The biggest challenge, Dunham says, is to be heard and taken seriously. That is a difficulty we all face to some degree. Everyone filters communication through their own lens of perception and experience. The differences that can strengthen us as a group can also divide us as individuals unless we make the effort to build relationships based on honor, integrity, and trust.

Dunham says that there are always temptations to cut corners in the choices she makes and the manner in which she relates to others. And that's the point; integrity in our relationships with others is a choice. Sometimes, it is a difficult choice that tests your resolve. Like the Scout who says, "On my honor, I will," integrity-driven leaders make and live by their commitment to doing what's right even when it is not convenient.

Dunham says, "When you live and lead your life with honor and integrity, most of your decisions are already made for you."

It is impossible to influence others over the long-term without being honorable and showing integrity in our interpersonal relations. You have to be authentic, open, and honest. You must honor others, build trust, and operate from a sense of service. And you must stay flexible without losing your principles.

A line from Shakespeare's *King Henry VI* says, "In thy face I see the map of honor, truth, and loyalty." That's what it takes to deal effectively with the souls of others. What do you choose to do?

CHAPTER FIVE

---- ✳ ----

MASTER THE COMPLEXITIES
OF ORGANIZATIONAL INTEGRITY

> *In my judgment, we shall win or lose the Age of*
> *Abundance to the degree that the businessman*
> *exhibits two virtues. The first is honesty—*
> *downright, old-fashioned truth telling. The second*
> *is that the businessman must have clear convictions*
> *about the kind of society, the kind of system they*
> *want, and they must be willing to stand up and*
> *fight for these convictions.*
>
> —HENRY R. LUCE

I MAGINE THIS: YOU (AN engineer) are a guest of a cabinet-level minister of a foreign government. The purpose of the visit is to close a multi-billion-dollar deal that is good for your host country, your company, and especially, your own career.

Only one thing stands between you and a plane ride home to accept the recognition that comes from closing a big deal. The minister wants you to make sure that a certain payment is made to a certain bank account. It's not a large payment. In fact, the request isn't for very much money at all. In this situation you would:

1. Make the payment.

2. Tell the minister that you are not allowed to make that decision and get his agreement to sign the deal pending the resolution of this small matter with your boss.

3. Hide the amount requested in the contract price for the agreement.

4. Work to convince the minister to accept another gift that could not be easily tracked.

5. Tell the minister that your company won't be able to do business with his country and leave the meeting.

The ethical answer is 5: Tell the minister that your company won't be able to do business with his country and leave the meeting. That is the answer you expect in a book about integrity in leadership. That is the answer a high percentage of CEOs, corporate ethics officers, and human resource professionals would want you to give.

The real answer, however, is likely to be "It depends."

A number of factors will influence your response to this dilemma: Are there laws that prohibit the request? Is this a routine course of action for your company? What is at stake for you personally? Will you secure a big promotion for landing this deal? Will you be fired for not landing it or fired for facilitating a bribe regardless of the law?

Let's take it one step further. Would your response be different if failing to complete this business agreement would bankrupt your company and put thousands of people out of work? What if the bonus you received for completing this deal would secure the special treatment your child needed for a debilitating disease?

WHAT THE NUMBERS SAY

In 2007, the Ethics Resource Center reported that 56 percent of all employees had personally observed behavior or misconduct that violates ethical standards, policy, or the law.[1] The significance of this statistic is two-fold:

1. The percentage of employees stating that they had seen questionable or illegal behavior was 55 percent in the year 2000, which was prior to Enron, WorldCom, and other corporate scandals that made headlines. Seven years later, that percentage has actually increased.

2. The United States passed the Sarbanes-Oxley Act in 2002, five years before this study, which would suggest that the law that was supposed to help ensure integrity and ethical behavior in organizations has not been as effective as many had hoped.

Employees are hesitant to report the misconduct that they observe for a variety of reasons, including fear of retaliation and cynicism that their actions would not make any difference.

Who can blame them for their reticence? Sherron Watkins, Cynthia Cooper, and Colleen Rowley were jointly selected as *Time* magazine's 2002 Person of the Year for their role in exposing, respectively, scandals at WorldCom and Enron, and the FBI's slow action prior to the attacks of September 11, 2001. Watkins and Cooper have moved on to successful careers as authors, consultants, and speakers. Rowley retired from the FBI after 24 years of service. These are the exception rather than the rule. Despite laws protecting whistleblowers, employees reporting misconduct are more likely to experience harassment, intimidation, poor performance reviews, and even termination.

The Ethics Resource Center report also revealed that the number of companies that have successfully created and sustained an ethical culture declined between 2005 and 2007 with only 9 percent of companies demonstrating strong ethical cultures.

The U.S. Department of Justice obtained nearly 1,300 fraud convictions between 2002 and 2008. This included convictions of more than

200 CEOs and corporate presidents; more than 120 corporate vice presidents, and more than 50 chief financial officers (CFOs).[2]

MORE NUMBERS

Still need more proof that integrity, honesty, and good-faith dealing are a challenge for today's organization? Look at these:

- A Gallup poll found that only 18 percent of U.S. adults reported "quite a lot" or "a great deal" of confidence in "big" business.[3]

- 83 percent of respondents to a poll conducted by TheLadders.com rated a company's business ethics as "very important" when deciding to take a job.[4]

- A study by LRN, a corporate ethics and compliance consulting firm, reported that 73 percent of U.S. full-time employees had observed ethical misconduct, and 10 percent "are aware of an issue that could create a scandal if discovered," 36 percent of those surveyed reported being distracted by the misconduct, and 46 percent told a coworker about it.[5]

It is not just business that has a problem. For example:

- 64 percent of high school students surveyed admitted to cheating on a test at least once in the past year.

- 82 percent said that they had copied another student's homework at least once in the past year.

- 59 percent of the students agreed that successful people do what it takes to win, even if others consider it cheating.[6]

- 57 percent of survey respondents believe that all or quite a few of the people who run for political office are "crooked."[7]

- Only 33 percent expressed "a great deal" or "quite a lot" of confidence in public schools.

- Only 24 percent expressed "a great deal" or "quite a lot" of confidence in television news.

- The percentage of people expressing "a great deal" or "quite a lot" of confidence for Congress, HMOs, and the criminal justice system, and organized religion came in at 12 percent, 13 percent, and 20 percent respectively.[8]

- 67 percent of Americans believed that religion was losing its influence in 2008.[9]

Perhaps a final vignette shows just how far we have fallen from ethical behavior: A mother in Garland, Texas, made national headlines when she fabricated an essay about why her six-year old daughter deserved to be awarded tickets to a Hannah Montana concert. The essay stated, "My daddy died this year in Iraq." Her justification was, "It said to write an essay. It never said it had to be true. I never said it was true. . . . It was just an essay. We wrote whatever we could to win."[10]

WHAT THE NUMBERS MEAN

Polls and surveys would lead you to believe that we are in the midst of an integrity crisis that threatens to destroy our entire way of life. The numbers cited here are exclusive to business in the United States, but anecdotal and statistical evidence points to the fact that Americans have not cornered the market on integrity challenges.

A second look at the state of integrity in our institutions and organizations reveals that while things are bad, current day scandals are not the first or necessarily the worst in our history; our cynicism is heavily influenced by what we see and hear over time; and organizational integrity is more complex today than ever.

HISTORY IN PERSPECTIVE

Singer/Songwriter Paul Simon wrote one of my favorite lines: "Every generation throws a hero up the pop charts."[11] And so it seems with scandals that shock our sensibilities and spur the clamor for a return to the traditional values of integrity and honesty—we get another one, traditionally, every fifteen to eighteen years.

Our anger over the Enrons, WorldComs, and Bernie Madoffs of the world is justified. But these weren't the first to try to pull a fast one on investors and customers. Long before the subprime mortgage scandals of 2008, there were the savings and loan crisis, the junk bond crisis, the insider trading crisis (more than once), and accounting scandals in every sector.

Executives at Beechnut, a large baby food company, were found guilty of selling phony apple juice.[12] Several companies were indicted for selling adulterated orange juice, apparently in full knowledge that it wasn't pure, because it increased their profit margins.[13] In one case, executives established an elaborate process for covering up their deceit by hiding the purchase of fraudulent ingredients, creating a secret room to add the ingredient to its product, falsifying records, and even attending a seminar on detecting adulterated products to pick up tips on hiding their conspiracy.[14] Executives at WorldCom and a host of other companies were found guilty of reporting phony revenue numbers and making fraudulent financial statements to get them a better price on their stock.[15] The products were different, but the fraud is the same.

Warner-Lambert agreed to pay $430 million to resolve charges for the illegal marketing of Neurontin[16] fourteen years after Bolar Pharmaceutical Company was forced by the FDA to remove from the market the largest-selling generic drug in America, a blood pressure medication taken by 500,000 people. Warner-Lambert, through its subsidiary Parke-Davis, marketed its drug for uses that had not been approved by the FDA. Bolar switched test samples to get the drug approved.[17]

The fraud convictions between 2002 and 2008 are impressive, and no doubt there are a few others that could or should have been prosecuted. However, there are approximately 15,000 publicly traded companies in the United States not to mention the number of private companies, sole proprietorships, charitable organizations, and churches.

A poll by the New York-based Edelman public relations firm actually showed trust in business increased between 2001 and 2007.[18] While trust in big business is low, trust in small business is markedly higher. Gallup Polls editor-in-chief, Frank Newport, says, "In polling, 'big' is an inflammatory negative. Ask Americans about small business, and they perk right up."[19]

We lament about the 67 percent who responded that religion is losing its influence until we compare it to 1970 when the percentage of people who believed religion was losing its influence reached 75 percent.[20]

Cheating in schools is certainly not new either. A 1986 study of 45 California sixth graders noted that 86 percent said that they had seen cheating. A 30-year longitudinal study by McCabe and Bowers revealed that college cheating was prevalent in 1962–1963.[21]

Government scandals and a loss of confidence are not new either. The Watergate cover up and subsequent resignation of Richard Nixon added a new phrase to the American lexicon. The word "gate" added to anything has become a shorthand label for scandal. There were lies, errors in judgment, and selective disclosure long before anyone became concerned by presidential comments such as "I never had sexual relations with that woman" or "We've found the weapons of mass destruction."

Ralph Keyes, in his book, *The Post-Truth Era,* summarizes our history with integrity and honesty: "As long as human beings have had words to say, they've said words that weren't true."[22]

Keyes elaborates by noting that, "Dishonesty inspires more euphemism than copulation or defecation."[23] And when you think about it, he is correct. When it comes to the truth, we embellish, expand, enrich, soften, shave, stretch, and withhold. We misspeak, pretend, bend, and improve. We are guilty of mistakes, misjudgment, and truthful hyperbole.

The integrity of our organizations and institutions is in question. Every indication is that dishonorable behavior is becoming an accepted aspect of every segment in our society, but let's not pretend that this is something new. Let's, also, not assume that there are no integrity-driven organizations left or that you can't be successful and have integrity.

WHAT CHANGED?

A television reporter asked me the following question during an interview about the technology bubble bursting and the accounting scandals that shook American business in 2002: "Have we learned our lesson?"

"It's too early to tell," I responded. "The true test will be what happens when our 401(k)s are earning 22 percent again."

It took less than six years to find out that some are willing to sacrifice integrity for short-term gain. The flattening of our world and organizations that has resulted from technology, globalization, and increased competition has made my previous comment about a scandal about once every generation obsolete.

Each new scandal is followed quickly, it seems, by another. Some of that can be attributed to the increase in population. But much of it, I believe, results from an increase in the number of people with whom we interact. The snake oil salesman appeared in his wagon maybe one time per year in the frontier days. The fraudulent e-mails about some Nigerian prince who needs my help with his frozen bank assets appear daily.

Mobility also plays a role. Living and working with the same group of people over a long period of time places a premium on establishing long-term relationships built on trust. The world we remember, and to some degree long for, was built on stability. The local establishment was deterred from predatory business practices because the owner had to live in the community. The "family name" was an important asset. The educator and the minister walked among us every day.

Migration and mobility patterns have made stable communities in which to live and work increasingly rare. Technology has broadened our reach, and it has reduced our connection to those with whom we are doing business. We exist in a world where connections to our neighbors have been replaced by connection to our Facebook, Twitter, and MySpace communities.

In cyberspace, you can be anyone you want to be. Some MySpace pages include sections where "friends" pledge total honesty implying that truthfulness is not required in other areas. Even the term *friend* has come to mean something different. I have a Facebook page with lots of "friends" who simply wanted to connect with me. I have never met them and will probably never do so.

The result is a cynicism that pervades our feelings about and trust in the organizations and institutions that define us.

The survey of students cited earlier in this chapter revealed several other important statistics:

- 98 percent believed that it is important to be a person with good character,

- 91 percent said their parents and guardians always want them to do what's right regardless of the cost, and

- 93 percent believe that trust and honesty are essential in personal relationships.[24]

We still believe traditional principles—integrity, honor, honesty, and trust—are important. We simply doubt that it makes a difference in achieving success.

WHY ORGANIZATIONAL INTEGRITY IS DIFFICULT

The connection between individual beliefs and behavior and the complexities of achieving organizational integrity is important. Our systems of religion, government, education, business, and even family rely on a sense of trust to effectively function. The systemic failures of our organizations and institutions are, in reality, a failure of individuals. Leaders chose, consciously or unconsciously, to enable an environment where doing what's right was sacrificed for expedience, greed, and desire for status.

The occurrences of misconduct are too numerous to write off as random acts, and they are not prevalent enough to issue a blanket indictment. Scandal paints with a broad roller rather than a fine brush. But experience points to the fact that there are as many, if not more, leaders who work tirelessly to promote integrity in their products, services, and relationships as there are those who make the headlines with scandal. There are five reasons why maintaining your organization's integrity is difficult today.

1. Pressure to Deliver Results in a Competitive Marketplace

"Winning isn't everything, winning is the only thing." This quote has come to symbolize the marketplace philosophy that the ends justify the means. There are the winners, and there is everyone else. The messages begin early in life and are reinforced in virtually every venue. Fathers pour illegal additives into the fuel of their seven-year-olds' midget racecars, and coaches knowingly allow an athlete to fabricate his age or address.[25]

Former GE CEO Jack Welch was cheered for the laser-like focus created by his statement that the company would be number one or number two in every market that it served. And yet, some people forget that Welch was equally adamant that delivering results without living the company's values was a recipe for extinction.

Former CitiGroup CEO Charles Prince, when asked about the perception that double-digit growth was the only acceptable level of performance, said, "I never thought you had to say to people, 'We want to grow aggressively—and don't forget not to break the law.'"[26] Prince's assertion that the vast majority of the company's 300,000 employees were not engaged in questionable activities to achieve earnings targets is correct. But, enough of them were involved to create multiple scandals that sullied the company's reputation.

2. Fear about Your Future Leads to Blind Loyalty

Betty Vinson is one of the tragic stories of the $11 billion accounting fraud perpetrated by WorldCom. She was asked by her superiors to make false accounting entries, resisted, and then gave in. For more than a year and a half she continued the illegal entries and ultimately helped to falsify $3.7 billion in profits.

A 2003 *Wall Street Journal* article described Vinson as the type of person most people would want to know and the type of employee most companies would want to have. She is the daughter of the former owner of a small typewriter shop. She is a mother, wife, and friend. Betty Vinson is, by all outward symbols, "a good person."

So how does someone with a reputation as hardworking and diligent turn into a convicted felon? A former colleague described her in the article as someone who would "do anything you told her." Yet, she knew that her actions were wrong. She and a few of her colleagues thought about quitting. She didn't. Vinson was the primary wage earner, and the family depended on her health insurance. Her concerns about entering the labor market as a middle-aged worker kept her at the company, committing illegal acts.[27]

Vinson was sentenced to five months in prison, five months of house arrest, and three years of probation. Fear and blind loyalty are not justification for Vinson's actions. They

> **Re-examine all that you have been told . . . dismiss that which insults your soul.**
>
> *—Walt Whitman*

are real challenges that all of us face in varying degrees during our lives. The personal integrity decision is to stand up for what is right regardless of the costs. The organizational integrity decision is to create the environment where fear and blind loyalty are not allowed to deter others from doing the same.

3. Lure of Expedience

Steroids can kill you—literally. Everyone knows it, and still steroid use exists at every level of athletic competition from high school to the professional ranks. Athletes can achieve many, if not most, of the same performance results they would on steroids through hard work and excellent nutrition. But that takes time, and our world is built on speed. We complain about the length of time it takes to microwave our meals. A two-minute report on the evening news is called an "in-depth analysis." Is it any wonder that we want immediate success?

The lure of expedience is the impatient version of the pressure to deliver results that was discussed earlier. The difference is that this one is based on greed rather than fear. Betty Vinson acted out of fear. The leaders at Enron acted out of greed. The result is the same—a willingness to cut corners to achieve success. It can be an out-of-control desire for external symbols of success or a feeling that you are behind others and need to catch up—either way, individuals and organizations caught up in the lure of expedience start down a slippery slope in which a return to the standards of integrity is difficult.

4. Poorly Designed Processes and Systems

Jayson Blair resigned from the *New York Times* in May 2003 after he was caught plagiarizing and, in some cases, completely fabricating parts of the stories he filed as legitimate news articles. Blair points to his diagnosis and successful treatment for bipolar disorder and history of drug use as contributing to his behavior. In this case, the cause is not the story because Blair had a history of questionable acts that were not identified or addressed by the *Times*. Accounts indicate that he was hired by the newspaper in January 1999 after falsely claiming that he completed his degree. Over the next several years, Blair was repeatedly criticized for various mistakes in his writing. His editor even requested that the *Times* management not allow Blair to continue writing for the newspaper. Management's response was to promote Blair to the national desk.

The *Times'* investigation into how and why Blair was allowed to continue, much less flourish, in his career as a journalist found a "series of management and operation breakdowns" and "a stunning lack of communication within the newsroom."[28] The internal processes and systems that should have identified and addressed problems early did not work. The result was a stunning slap in the face for one of the world's most trusted news sources.

5. The Impact of the Culture

An organization's or a society's culture is the essence of what that group believes is important. Cultures are a powerful tool for creating a sense of connection among the members. In organizations like Enron, bending the rules became laudable. Watercooler conversations, promotions, and public recognition confer star status on those who produce the big payday.

At a broader level, the current culture not only expects dishonesty, it rewards it with movie contracts, book deals, and media appearances. Cheating is carried as a badge of honor. Prior to being named the number-one player in the 2008 National Football League draft, Jake Long said: "I'll admit that I hold. . . . It's a skill. If you can get away with it and not get caught, it's absolutely a skill. I try to make sure I get my hands inside on every single play, so if I do hold, the refs won't be able to see it."[29]

Bob Corbett even wrote a book that celebrates our acceptance of less-than-honorable behavior, *The Cheater's Handbook: The Naughty Student's Bible*. The book provides information on a variety of strategies and tactics such as the timing for eating a cheat sheet and how to invent footnotes.[30] I expect that at least part of the motivation for writing this book is the comic relief it provides. And those who know me well will attest that I would find much of this subject laugh-out-loud funny. Nevertheless, our willing acceptance that cheating is worth any sort of recognition says something about our culture.

Keyes calls it the "routinization of dishonesty."[31] I view it as mass application of Sir Henry Taylor's famous quote:

Falsehood ceases to be falsehood when it is understood on all sides that the truth is not expected to be spoken.

Either way, the choice to go along and get along is often easier than standing for one's values.

THERE ARE THOSE WHO GET IT RIGHT

Any one of the five factors just discussed would make achieving integrity in our organizations difficult. Combine all five, and you begin to understand how difficult it is for leaders to instill a culture of integrity in products, services, and relationships in their organizations. Yet, there are those who stand out. They are not perfect, they are not weak or soft, and they are not void of a sense of humor. They simply understand that our organizations and institutions define our relationships with others and that those relationships are vital to lasting success. Here are some things to look for to help you spot organizational integrity in practice. The organization:

- Makes every decision—new product design, marketing, business development, employee relations, customer service, sales strategies, accounts payable schedules, contributions to charitable organizations, and everything else that comes up in the organization—on the basis of what's right rather than who's right.

- Provides quality products and services while embracing continuous improvement in all performance areas. These organizations seek to deliver on the promise of their brand every day.

- Maintains a culture where ethical behavior and doing what is right is expected and rewarded.

- Operates in an open, transparent manner with all constituencies.

- Delivers on promises (implied and explicit) to all constituent groups.

- Complies with the spirit of applicable regulations rather than the minimum requirements.

- Ensures accountability for integrity at every level of the organization.

As a result, the organization experiences:

- Enhanced brand loyalty and reputation;

- Increased morale, commitment, and productivity;

- Improved resource utilization;

- Confidence in compliance with laws and regulations; and

- More effective responses to crisis situations.

The results speak for themselves. A study by Watson Wyatt Worldwide found that companies with a high trust level among employees posted 42 percent higher shareholder returns.[32] Eighty-two percent of consumers have stopped using a company's products when trust is broken according to the *Harris Poll*.[33]

THE REST OF THE STORY

The case presented at the beginning of this chapter is real. The young engineer was Rex Tillerson, current chairman and CEO of ExxonMobil.

Tillerson told me that he spent the twelve-hour flight home worrying that he would get fired for losing the deal. On his return, he told a member of the company's management committee what had happened and that he had walked away. The management committee member's response was, "That's fine. You did the right thing."

Thirty days later, Tillerson received a letter from the offending minister inviting him back to the country. The two parties re-engaged on the negotiation and the subject of an "outside" payment never came up again.

INTEGRITY AT EXXONMOBIL

I interviewed Rex Tillerson during the summer of 2008. Oil prices were at record highs, the company was reporting record earnings, and both the U.S. media and Congress were making accusations about the behavior of oil companies and oil company executives.

Tillerson told me that ExxonMobil's reputation around the world is strong. The company is highly respected by government leaders worldwide. He acknowledged that the company is described by its partners as being "difficult to work with" but "whatever they tell you, you can take it to the bank."

To Tillerson, results are important, but what is more important is the way those results are achieved. He says that's what determines your ultimate success and future value to the company.

So how about those record profits? How can you both operate with integrity and earn so much money? I asked.

"We've been at this 125 years," Tillerson responded. "You don't stay around for 125 years without having a commitment to very high standards of conduct."

"If we weren't ethical and honest in our dealings," he continued, "we couldn't produce those kinds of results because success would be so fleeting. You only have to look at failed companies and failed leaders in situations where they made a lot of money for a short period of time because their business wasn't built on a solid foundation of integrity and ethical behavior."[34]

An Important Distinction

Shortly after my conversation with Tillerson, a friend commented that he just didn't buy what Tillerson was saying. He just couldn't reconcile the idea of a company making that much money and still claiming to be integrity-driven in its culture and approach.

I countered with ExxonMobil's long and distinguished list of accomplishments and support of socially responsible initiatives. I told him how the company had led the fight to solve the malaria problem in Africa; invested $125 million as the founders of the National Math and Science Initiative in the United Sates; and gave away $225 million in 2008 through its charitable and community programs. ExxonMobil employees donated over 690,000 hours in volunteer efforts in 2008.

My friend still wasn't buying my argument, and we parted agreeing to disagree. The distinction between our views is important: Each of us views and interprets integrity through our own lens of perception.

Acting with integrity, being honest, and operating ethically are not an insurance policy that guarantees everyone will like and agree with you. It does not free you from having to perform in a competitive marketplace or from making difficult business decisions. The major oil companies have been investigated over thirty times by the Federal Trade Commission without a single finding of collusion or violation of rules or regulations.

Important decisions such as when and where to drill for oil and where to locate refineries are made many years, sometimes decades, in advance. Tillerson and his staff are smart people, but they cannot predict with a finite degree of certainty what the price of oil is going to be in five or six years; what steps the government in a country will take that either expands or decreases availability; or what the global economy is going to do to prices. Operating from a foundation of integrity, as Exxon-Mobil has proven, allows you to stay in business for a very long time in a very challenging market by building and sustaining relationships built on trust. Tillerson summed it up this way, "We always try to be truthful and aboveboard. We don't have anything to hide."

It is obvious why a company like ExxonMobil must pay constant attention to integrity. It has 80,000 employees in countries throughout the world, with almost 65 percent of those employees working outside of the United States. Its operation is based on sustaining relationships with governments and partners around the world. A failure to protect the company's reputation by even 1 or 2 percent of those employees can have a significant and lasting impact.

But what if your organization is significantly smaller? The challenges Tillerson faces are no different from those facing any other leader: How to create alignment throughout the organization; how to ensure people do the right things the right way and for the right reasons; and how to build a culture where integrity and accountability are viewed as valued tools for long-term sustainability and growth.

AN EXECUTIVE WHO GETS IT

Money magazine ranked Carrollton, Texas, number 15 on its 2008 list of best small cities in which to live. This community has just over 120,000 in population and occupies 37 square miles in northwest Dallas County.

On the surface, Carrollton is similar to many suburban communities throughout the United States. Dig a little deeper, and you find a municipal government operation marked by a commitment to efficiency and effectiveness. Staffing has decreased from 939 positions in 1995 to 843 positions in 2009 even though the population has increased by over 25 percent. Leading the charge to transform the culture is Leonard Martin, the city manager, who operates as the organization's CEO.

Carrollton's organization is a great case study for my book, *Results Rule!* (Hoboken, NJ: Wiley, 2006). In a profession where the business model is often an either/or decision to raise taxes or lower service, Carrollton has decided to change the game.

With results like these, it is easy to understand why the Carrollton City Council considered adjusting Martin's compensation in 2007. He was being paid approximately 20 percent less than his peers while delivering superior results.

Martin turned down the increase. He told the Council that he could not in good conscience take the salary adjustment being offered while telling his employees that the City could only afford a 4 percent pay raise for them. He agreed to additional nonrevenue benefits such as time off instead.

In contrast, there are countless examples of those in power choosing self-interest over the path of integrity and credibility. Banks receiving financial assistance from the U.S. federal government in 2009 had to be restrained from using the money to pay executive bonuses. Investment bank executives took severance payouts in the millions of dollars while employees and investors walked away with nothing.

Executives with compensation packages matched only in size by their egos are acting within a legal contract. In these cases, the boards of directors have failed to exercise prudence and restraint.

It doesn't have to be that way. Executives could step up and be leaders. Leonard Martin did it, and he makes a lot less than the corporate executives who make the headlines.

There are integrity-driven leaders in every walk of life who would make the same decision as Martin. What would you do? And most important, who would you want to lead the organization where you work?

YOU DON'T HAVE TO BE BIG—INTEGRITY AT CMA

RTI/Community Management Associates, Inc. (CMA) received the 2006 American Business Ethics Award, and yet it doesn't really have a formal ethics program. What it does have is an unyielding commitment to living its values, and in doing so, CMA has developed a reputation for integrity in its products, services, and relationships.

Judi Phares, CMA's CEO, teamed up with a partner to open the company in 1983. Today the company has approximately 125 employees and services over 190 homeowner associations representing over 74,000 individual owners.

From the beginning, living by a strong set of values has been the driving force behind CMA's operating principles. Phares's vision is to set the standard for excellence in performance and reputation in the industry. It is a passion that was instilled from her parents and reinforced by seeing what does and doesn't work in building strong, sustainable organizations. Phares says the desire came from her previous experience working in a company where integrity and doing what's right consistently took a backseat to making a quick profit.

Over the years, Phares and CMA have found that a commitment to integrity can make it more difficult to compete, but she wouldn't have it any other way. She says, "In our business, there is a tendency for people to focus on the cost of a service rather than its quality. And, our costs are often a little higher than some of our competitors. That's because we don't take shortcuts. We provide more service; we invest in technology; and we pay people well by industry standards. We strive to make sure that the contractors we use at our client's property operate with high standards. When there is a choice between doing what's right and making a short-term profit, we do what's right. For instance, some companies might charge $15 to mow a yard. But the person doing the work may not be wearing safety glasses or shoes and may not be supervised on the site. We will recommend that our clients pay a few dollars more to get the extra level of quality and assurance they deserve."[35]

While it might cost more in the short-term, CMA's results over the long-term prove that doing what's right pays dividends. The company's ROI is typically higher than its competitors, and its customer loyalty is outstanding. Four of the company's five original management contracts are still managed by CMA twenty-six years later.

THE CMA VALUES

CMA has built a reputation for professionalism. The company trains all employees to know and understand its core values, which are built around respect for the individual, honesty, and the belief that knowledge, education, and experience are invaluable. The values are:

- We respect the individual and believe that individuals who are treated with respect and given responsibility respond by giving their best.
- We require complete honesty and integrity in everything we do.
- We make commitments with care and then live up to them. In all things, we do what we say we are going to do.
- Work is an important part of life, and it should be fun. Being a good businessperson does not mean being stuffy and boring.
- We are frugal. We guard and conserve the company's, as well as each association's resources with at least the same vigilance that we would use to guard and conserve our own personal resources. (Actually more!)
- We insist on giving our best effort in everything we undertake. Furthermore, we see a huge difference between "good mistakes" (best effort, bad result) and "bad mistakes" (sloppiness or lack of effort).
- Clarity in understanding our mission, our goals, and what we expect from each other is critical to our success.
- We are believers in the Golden Rule. In all our dealings we will strive to be friendly and courteous, as well as fair and compassionate.
- We feel a sense of urgency on any matters related to our clients. We own problems, and we are always responsive. We are client driven.
- We support and encourage individuals who desire to continue their education.

- We believe in charity of the heart.
- We support the concept of team.[36]

MAKING INTEGRITY A WAY OF LIFE

ExxonMobil and CMA are about as different as any two companies can be. Yet, conversations with Tillerson and Phares reveal many similarities in their concerns and their approach to mastering the complexities of organizational integrity.

In both cases, the decision to make integrity the cornerstone of the organization's operation begins with the leader and is driven throughout the organization by performance and execution. Tillerson and Phares both live and lead by the principle that how results are achieved is, in the long run, just as—if not more—important than the results themselves. Both leaders embrace their responsibility to build sustainable organizations that can be trusted by everyone with whom they come in contact. And both Tillerson and Phares understand that maintaining a reputation for integrity in products, services, and relationships requires constant attention. There are seven strategies that you can take from these very different and equally effective leaders to use in making integrity a way of life.

1. State Your Expectations Clearly

Tillerson says, "We operate in an environment where the rules of the game are different in each part of the world, but the rules for our people are the same every day." ExxonMobil has a written set of principles for business conduct that covers ethics, transparency, and integrity that enable success regardless of the environment in which you are operating. Employees receive a copy of the principles during orientation and go through regularly scheduled retraining. At CMA, the process is similar. Employees are provided a copy of the company's values at hiring. Phares attends every employee orientation program to discuss the CMA values, her expectations for staff, and the expectations staff should have of her.

2. Pay Attention to Processes and Alignment

Tillerson says, "The leader doesn't do anything other than set the alignment for the organization." Much of that alignment comes through an individual leader's actions and words. The best organizations take that a step further by ensuring alignment between operating processes and organizational principles and values.

Processes create habits that ensure consistency. CMA builds their values into every process—including the process they use to develop processes. Every policy, procedure, and even the company mission was built by teams of employees in line with the company values to support the concept of team and to help create ownership. ExxonMobil, like CMA, builds performance aligned with the company's principles and values into performance reviews, promotion decisions, and selection processes. Each year ExxonMobil employees sign a statement stating that they have read the company's operating principles, that they understand them, that they have done nothing in the past year inconsistent with those principles, and that they will do nothing to violate them in the future.

Everything is ultimately connected. Deceptive marketing practices influence attitudes and behavior in other departments. Allowing disrespectful treatment of employees in one area will eventually affect other areas. The integrity of the whole is called into question when people see inconsistencies among the various parts. To ensure alignment and integrity, the leader must ask the following three questions of each area of the business:

Are we doing what we said we would do?

Are we providing what we said we would provide?

Are we operating in a manner that builds trust in our products, services, and relationships?

3. Create Accountability and Rewards

People must see that acting with integrity means something. Deal quickly with those who violate the organization's standards. Fear of consequences can create an environment where individuals work to avoid getting caught. Make honoring commitments and the ability to build trust among diverse groups criteria for promotion. Recognize and reward those who demonstrate their integrity in a difficult situation, even when the result is not as you would have hoped. Behavior that is recognized is repeated.

Tillerson spoke to me about the "very bright line" that exists for upholding the company's principles about ethics, transparency, and integrity:

It is a very bright line in our company, and the consequences are harsh when it is crossed. More often than not, it involves termination. These can be the smallest of things—someone decides to pay for a personal meal with their corporate credit card. Perhaps they left their personal card at home or were maxed out on their credit, and they say, 'I'll just pay you back later.' That's a violation of our policy. You have to get permission to do that, and if you don't follow that rule, you can be fired.

It is no different at CMA. Phares says: "It is very simple. We try to hire people who share our values. And, we hold people accountable when they don't." She goes on to say:

> *Distinguishing between intentional mistakes and honest errors is part of our values. I can't tell you that we have a perfect method for distinguishing between the two, but after we have researched the facts, we watch a staff member's reaction when confronted. If the person is crushed and it is obvious that something was not done intentionally, we are more likely to give them another chance. But, there are times in life when you have to draw the line and stand for something. If there is a question about their integrity, they are not likely to get a second chance.*

Likewise, CMA and ExxonMobil make sure that living their principles and values is rewarded. Tillerson described the commitment this way:

> *Results are important, but what's more important to us—and what we're going to judge you on more keenly in terms of your success and value in the future—is how you got those results. We emphasize that everywhere we go.*

4. Provide the Skills and Tools to Put Principles into Practice

CMA links every education and training activity, from new employee orientation to the company's new software system, to the value system. Every ExxonMobil employee hears about the company's operating principles at employee orientation and goes through retraining on a scheduled basis. The commitment to provide education, skill building, and tools to help others know and apply the principles and values of your organization reinforces their importance and increases the organization's capacity for success.

5. Talk about Integrity Often

How often do you speak about your organization's key performance results? How often do you speak about the fact that success is ultimately based on the integrity of your products, services, and relationships?

Leaders, like Tillerson and Phares, who understand the value and complexities of earning a reputation for integrity talk about it often. Phares talks about the company's values as she walks the halls of CMA interacting with staff and at the monthly Breakfast Round Table where randomly chosen staff attend to discuss company issues and the company's stance. She encourages employees to challenge her when they have a question or perceive some inconsistency between her actions and the CMA values. And, the CMA leadership challenges both their staff and each other on a regular basis.

There are many leaders who would feel insulted or perhaps threatened by an employee questioning a decision or action. Tillerson and Phares expect and appreciate it. Phares told me, "I love it. It shows that people understand and embrace the value system."

Tillerson sets aside time to speak with employees and answer questions in every stop as he travels the globe. Questions about why decisions were made and actions taken are normal, expected, and appreciated. Tillerson understands that every interaction is an opportunity to teach how the company's principles affect every day decisions.

Hanging a values statement on the wall and distributing wallet cards are not enough. Very few take the time to pull out the card and review the values statement when they face a difficult choice. However, they will remember the stories and legends about those who achieved superior results while modeling integrity. Talk about the challenges of earning and maintaining the trust of others. The more attention you give to the value of integrity as a competitive tool, the more important it will become in the organization.

6. Welcome Bad News

The test of a healthy organization is not the absence of problems. It is the ability to address them in a positive manner.

The story of Betty Vinson mentioned earlier is what happens when someone feels trapped by a powerful boss and a decision that would ultimately affect their own livelihood and that of others. Vinson wasn't alone in this feeling. Dozens of WorldCom employees knew about the fraud that was taking place and did not speak out because of fear.[37]

It is easy to understand and empathize over Vinson's case. There are powerful leaders who intimidate, manipulate, and even bully employees to do what everyone knows is wrong.

Integrity-driven companies are different. The expectation is that no manager would ever ask an employee to engage in this type of behavior. And they would create vehicles to welcome bad news just in case a problem behavior slipped through.

Tillerson told me that one or two people can create a situation from which it takes months or even years to recover. That is why ExxonMobil has well-publicized procedures for raising questions or sharing concerns.

It is less formal but just as important at CMA. Phares says, "We want employees to feel that they can come to any leader, ask questions, and challenge us."

The permission to share bad news without fear of retribution promotes an honest, open environment that continually strives to improve. As good as your organization is today, there is a strong chance that someone is withholding information that can make it even better. Remember—truth is the victim when we value the illusion of success. Integrity-driven leaders and cultures focus on what is real.

7. Don't Forget Personal Leadership

Leaders live in a fishbowl. Everything they do is open for analysis, interpretation, and comment. It doesn't matter if your organization is 80,000
employees in countries throughout the world like ExxonMobil or 125
employees in a single geographic area. Tillerson and Phares understand
and embrace this.

Tillerson observed, "When I make a decision, I know the organization will be closely watching and interpreting the decision and our standards." He went on to say, "You are always on. You never have the luxury
of having an off moment or an off day."

Phares reached the same conclusion, "There is not a moment in my
life at CMA when I am not cognizant that the actions I am taking are
being watched and evaluated."

Leadership, at its core, has very little to do with position, and yet position matters. People obstruct justice every day, but it is different when
the president of the United States or the CEO of a company does it.
People lie on a regular basis, but the falsehood takes on an entirely different meaning when it comes from an individual in position of authority
or influence. Others are watching. They judge our actions through their
own lens of perception. They will take their support elsewhere unless
they see integrity in our performance.

HOW ABOUT THE LEGAL STUFF?

Professions and industries find themselves regulated by others when they fail
to regulate themselves. The Sarbanes-Oxley Act of 2002 is the most prominent
example as the U.S. federal government sought to make it more difficult for
publicly traded companies to "cook the books."

The Sarbanes-Oxley Act is 66 pages long and covers important topics
such as reporting of financial statements, codes of ethics for senior officers,
corporate tax returns, and establishing internal controls. There are eleven ti-

tles within the Act with the majority of the compliance issues contained in six of the sections. There is no shortage of excellent accountants and consultants to help your company understand and implement the provisions of this law.

More important, however, is a little-known document called the "Federal Sentencing Guidelines." Published in 1991, these guidelines tell judges how to punish people for crimes such as fraud, cooking the books, polluting the environment, and a host of other infractions that most people would consider lacking in integrity.

For years, these guidelines were applied mostly to large companies. However, in 2004 the guidelines were changed to apply to all companies—public or private—regardless of size. The guidelines state explicitly that companies are to "promote an organizational culture that encourages ethical conduct and a commitment to compliance with the law."[38]

These guidelines are not about the law, however. They are really a way to protect your organization should someone be found guilty of breaking the law. Think of it as the "how to minimize my risk in case someone does something stupid" guidelines. There are five things you need to do to minimize your risk:

1. Create and communicate a formal, written ethics policy, and train your staff on how to use it.

2. Assign high-level personnel who do not have a history of engaging in illegal activity with the responsibility of ensuring compliance.

3. Take reasonable steps to monitor and audit compliance with the law including a system that allows your staff to report misconduct without fear of retribution.

4. Take consistent and appropriate enforcement action to address both misconduct and the failure to detect misconduct.

5. Take all reasonable steps to respond to an offense and prevent it from happening in the future.[39]

Regulations are the minimum standards. Following them allows you to say that you are not breaking the law. Integrity-driven leaders hold themselves and their organizations to a higher standard. By the time you get to illegal, you have traveled way past the standards of integrity, honor, and trust.

Five Components of an Effective Ethics Policy

1. *Organizational philosophy and commitment to ethical operation:* A statement of the organization's commitment to ethical business practices including any special considerations that apply in that specific environment. These are often stated as core values.

2. *Fiduciary responsibility statement:* Fiduciary responsibilities to act in the organization's best interest for officers and staff.

3. *Code of conduct:* The established standard of behavior for officers and employees. Codes of conduct may be general in nature or include clear requirements about specific acceptable behavior including:

   - Nondiscrimination
   - Conflict of interest
   - Acceptance of gifts and travel
   - Confidentiality
   - Accuracy and completeness of records
   - Commitment to follow laws and regulations
   - Transparency of transactions and relationships
   - Post-employment or service restrictions
   - Nepotism
   - Improper use of position
   - Improper use of resources
   - Limits on financial interest
   - Expected behavior in meetings and while performing official duties
   - Other policies regarding professional behavior as developed by the organization

4. *Education, investigation, and enforcement:* A strong, independent process should be developed to:

   - Investigate complaints
   - Issue advisory opinions

- Provide education and training
- Determine the appropriate action when problems are discovered

5. *Protection for whistle-blowers:* Individuals who view activities that violate the organization's policies must be encouraged to come forward and they must be protected from retribution or other negative consequences when they do so.

What If You Mess Up?

Mistakes happen. Some mistakes are made in an attempt to do what is right. Some are intentional efforts to deceive. Some can best be explained by this statement: Stupid has its own momentum.

Risk management experts will rightfully tell you to be careful of what you say and do. Any statement or action can be used as an admission of guilt that has significant implications. Alternatively, honor and integrity dictate that you take responsibility for your actions. Here are three steps to take when you find yourself or your organization in the position of having to respond to a crisis situation or mistake:

1. **Admit it and own up to it if you did it.** It is not enough to say you are sorry. Everyone can spot a fake, insincere apology a mile away. If you did it, admit it. Don't use weasel words. Don't be arrogant, and don't think that position, status, or circumstances make you special. You shouldn't take responsibility for something you didn't do, and don't admit to something if the facts are in question. You know if what you did was wrong. Admit it and accept the bad press that will come from it. You earn more respect by being honest.

2. **Act on it.** Don't just apologize for the mistake, do something about it. Do something to correct the situation or mitigate the

effects. Do something to make sure that this type of problem never happens again. In January 1988, Ashland Oil Company dumped 3.9 million gallons of diesel fuel into the Monongahela River outside of Pittsburgh, Pennsylvania. The prosecutor in the case sought to obtain $8 million in damages, double the amount allowed by the Clean Water Act, because of the number of mistakes and violations that occurred. Ashland, however, was given a much lower fine of $2.25 million because the judge found that the company had done everything that it could to make restitution and correct the situation.[40]

3. **Move on, but don't forget.** Thanks to digital technology and the Internet, the smallest of errors can end up broadcast around the world in a matter of minutes. Every cell phone with a movie or camera feature makes you a potential star at the most inopportune time. Every person with a blog or social media account is an investigative reporter looking to break an interesting story. The mistakes we make eventually recede from public discussion, but they never completely go away. That is an unfortunate consequence of living in a connected world. You, on the other hand, must move on. Becoming shackled by the past helps no one. It is essential, however, that the lessons never recede from memory. We have all witnessed the truth in Sir Winston Churchill's statement, "Those who fail to learn from history are doomed to repeat it."

JOHNSON & JOHNSON: INTEGRITY IN A CRISIS

Johnson & Johnson's actions during the Tylenol crisis in 1982 have become the classic example of how to respond with integrity in the face of crisis. Seven people died when an individual—not an employee—tampered with Tylenol capsules in the Chicago area. Blame was not attributed to Johnson & Johnson, but the company voluntarily pulled the product off the shelves and kept it off until they had developed tamper-resistant packaging. Fortunately for Johnson & Johnson, they not only did the right thing, they were perceived as having done the right thing. The company suffered a short-term loss in profits, but their immediate sense of duty to their customers and the public resulted in a long-term increase in Tylenol's market share.

Johnson & Johnson didn't have to wonder how to react when the crisis came, they had a corporate credo crafted in 1943 to guide them. The credo established the company's priorities and defined its duties and responsibilities:

We believe our first responsibility is to the doctors, nurses, and patients, to mothers and all others who use our products and services. In meeting their needs, everything we do must be of high quality. We must constantly strive to reduce our costs in order to maintain reasonable prices. Customers' orders must be serviced promptly and accurately. Our suppliers and distributors must have an opportunity to make a fair profit.

We are responsible to our employees, the men and women who work with us throughout the world. Everyone must be considered as an individual. We must respect their dignity and recognize their merit. They must have a sense of security in their jobs. Compensation must be fair and adequate, and working conditions, clean, orderly, and safe. Employees must feel free to make suggestions and complaints. There must be equal opportunity for employment, development, and advancement for those qualified. We must provide competent management, and their actions must be just and ethical.

We are responsible to the communities in which we live and work and to the world community as well. We must be good citizens—support good works and charities and bear our fair share of taxes. We must encourage civic improvements and better health and education. We must maintain in good order the property we are privileged to use, protecting the environment and natural resources.

Our final responsibility is to our stockholders. Business must make a sound profit. We must experiment with new ideas. Research must be carried on, innovative programs developed, and mistakes paid for. New equipment must be purchased, new facilities provided, and new products launched. When we operate according to these principles, the stockholders should realize a fair return.[41]

    Johnson & Johnson went above and beyond their duty to act. They were honest with the media, with the government, with the consumers—and both the people and the press appreciated it. The company saw its market share drop from 35 percent of the pain reliever market to 8 percent immediately after the 1982 crisis. And then saw market share rebound in less than a year.[42] A leading factor in the recovery was Johnson & Johnson's integrity. It chose to follow its Credo rather than leave it as a feel-good example of corporate good intention.

    Contrast this with the actions of manufacturer A.H. Robins: In 1974, after three years of aggressive marketing and $2.86 million in sales. A.H. Robins stopped selling its Dalkon Shield intrauterine device in the United States. By then, the evidence was mounting that the shield was life threatening to users. Rather than recall product, Robins (and its subsequent owner) fought its responsibility in court—challenging victims' claims—for over ten years.[43] Reports also indicate that Robins knew that the original research around the product was suspect,[44] and it continued to cite that research in its marketing after the device's dangers were discovered.[45] It is little wonder that U.S. District Judge Miles Lord called the A.H. Robins' conduct, "This is corporate irresponsibility at its meanest."[46]

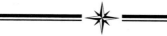

Fortune magazine author Kenneth Labich wrote: "As this economic slowdown lingers like some stubborn low-grade infection, managers are putting the heat on subordinates. Many of the old rules no longer seem to apply."

    The article goes on to reference middle managers who write deceptive reports, frontline employees who tell the boss what she wants to hear; product recalls for shoddy standards and practices, and all sorts of misrepresentations and deceit.

The statements could have been ripped from the headlines as the economic crisis of 2008 and 2009 unfolded. And yet, it was written in April 1992.[47]

Labich points to the good news: Over 40 percent of the Fortune 1,000 were holding ethics training sessions. About one-third had established an ethics committee.[48] And yet, the challenges of operating with integrity continued. The Sarbanes-Oxley Act was supposed to make a difference. It didn't. We were supposed to learn from the accounting fraud scandals of 2001–2002. We didn't—just as we didn't after the Ponzi Scheme of 1920, the insider trading and savings and loan crisis of the 1980s, or any of the accounting scandals of the 1990s.

You can't regulate organizational integrity. You must lead to it. It's a complex and difficult job, and if your goal is to build a sustainable and enduring organization that earns and maintains the trust of others, it's worth the effort.

CHAPTER SIX

Traditional Principles and Twenty-First Century Challenges

> *A society without respect for its leaders is a society*
> *ready to disintegrate.*
>
> —CHARLES HANDY

W HO DO YOU TRUST? Or more specifically, who *can* you trust? It is the most pressing leadership question of our day, and the importance of finding an answer increases exponentially as uncertainty grows in our world. The ability of leaders to earn and maintain the trust, credibility, and respect of followers will determine our ability to meet the challenges and seize the opportunities with which we are presented.

THE SCOPE OF THE CREDIBILITY PROBLEM

Institutions that have traditionally defined how we perceive and interact with the world in which we live include the family, religion or the church, the government, the education system, and business.

The headlines scream with examples of leaders in each who have failed to meet our standards for character, competence, consistency, communication, and courage. Business leaders bend—and often break—the rules while being irresponsible with other peoples' money. Financial gurus miss the pending train wreck in the economy. Political leaders put partisanship before principle. "Role models" in sports and entertainment find themselves as the lead stories for media outlets of all types as they prove that irresponsible behavior and self-sabotage show no limits of good taste, common sense, or morality.

You can rationalize it as an unintended consequence of a media-driven world that feeds on scandal. You can blame it on the destruction of the nuclear family, declining moral values in the home, the failure of our education system, Wall Street greed, or whichever political party happens to be in power at the time. Or, you can do something to influence the future.

THREE WHO CHOSE TO LEAD

History is filled with references to individuals who chose to influence the future rather than step aside and accept the status quo—from William Wallace, the commoner who united the Scots to overthrow British rule in the thirteenth century to the founding fathers of the United States; from Booker T. Washington and W.E.B. Du Bois to Harriett Tubman, Mary McLeod Bethune, and Rosa Parks; from Nobel Prize winner and physicist Luis Walter Alvarez to Nobel Prize nominee, writer, and labor organizer Ernesto Galarza. Every country, culture, and generation has its leaders. Some are known to everyone. Most are known to only a few. Here are three examples of everyday leaders who made a difference because they cared enough to do something.

Bill Strickland

Frank Ross's high school art room was a place of innovation, learning, and enthusiasm—a powerful contrast to the experience Bill Strickland had come to know growing up in Manchester, an inner-city neighbor-hood of Pittsburgh, Pennsylvania. Strickland was struck by his teach-er's artistic and technical ability with ceramics. The experience cap-tured his imagination, provided a sense of hope, and changed his life.

Strickland's student-teacher relationship with Ross gave form to the future vision of the Manchester Craftsmen's Guild (MCG). The Guild began as an after-school arts program in a donated North Side row house that Strickland secured while still a college student at the University of Pittsburgh.

Strickland told me that there were a number of people trying dif-ferent things to change communities in the 1960s. His idea to utilize the arts—initially ceramics and photography—resonated with the com-munity. It was a great vision shared and aided by many in the commu-nity combined with Strickland's determination that allowed the MCG to flourish while other programs faltered. Based on his success there, Strick-land was asked to assume leadership of Pittsburgh's Bidwell Training Center (BTC) in 1971.

Today, Manchester Bidwell Corporation is a model for educa-tion, culture, and hope. It serves over 3,900 youth each year through classes and workshops in ceramics, photography, digital imaging, and design art at the MCG. The MCG Jazz program is an anchor of the Pittsburgh community by bringing national and international jazz art-ists together with students and the community. The BTC provides market-driven career education created through strong partner-ships with leading local industries. The center offers accredited As-sociates Degree and diploma programs in fields as varied as culinary arts, chemical laboratory technologies, health care, horticulture, and office technology.

I asked Strickland what he now knows that he wishes he had known before. He responded without hesitation: (1) how a vision for providing hope can transform individual lives and communities, and (2) his own ability to do world-class things. Strickland is working toward his goal of replicating the success of the MCG and BTC in 200 centers around the world. His work and leadership are included as case studies at Harvard Business School where he serves as a guest lecturer.

Bill Strickland knows that ideal circumstances are not required to take responsibility and control of your life. He briefly worked as an airline pilot before being laid off when Braniff airlines went into bankruptcy. It turns out that the decision made under Howard Putnam's leadership (see Chapter 3) created the opportunity and confidence for Strickland to expand his work at the MCG and BTC.

The lessons of passion, hope, integrity, and responsibility are central to the educational experience Strickland and his team delivers. The goal is to turn out well-trained individuals who bring good values and citizenship to their lives, relationships, and communities. Strickland believes that we can manufacture hope in our time. What is required is our willingness and ability to see ourselves and others as valuable contributors and then take small steps to turn that idea into action.

John Montgomery

Bridgeway Capital Management, the company that John Montgomery founded in 1993, is a quantitative investment management firm that uses proprietary statistical models to create investment portfolios designed to outperform their targeted benchmarks. That means Montgomery is a very smart person.

But, that's not why you need to know about him. Every Bridgeway employee is a "Partner." But, that's not unusual either. Many companies call their staff members by names such as partner, associate, or crew member. Bridgeway, however, is unique because it actually treats people as partners by giving everyone input into a host of decisions that are traditionally reserved for those with managerial responsibility. It is a nonhierarchical culture where process and results take precedent over title and status. No Bridgeway partner is allowed to make more than seven times the salary of the lowest paid partner.

Montgomery's desire to build a different kind of company doesn't stop there. Bridgeway Capital Management commits one-half of its after-tax profits annually to philanthropic endeavors. Through its Foundation, Bridgeway advocates core issues such as peace and reconciliation, human rights, and eliminating genocide. It also supports broader issues related to early education, higher education, international humanitarian aid and relief, and the Houston community.

As a teenager, Montgomery realized that genocide and ethnic cleansing are a contemporary reality. Today, he translates this in a more graphic and disturbing way. "With media bringing news immediately to our televisions, new economic ties, and now the Internet, we no longer have the excuse of distance or lack of knowledge." Montgomery often wondered how neighbors in Nazi Germany could stand by and do nothing during the Holocaust. His concerns about how unconscionable behavior could be tolerated ignited a passion to see genocide end during his lifetime. "The neighbor has become—myself," he says. "And I realized I wasn't really doing anything about it."

Anne Ream

Anne Ream is a former executive with Leo Burnett, USA, one of the country's largest and best-known advertising and communications firms, who now works as a writer and creative director in Chicago. She is also a rape survivor.

Ream had no examples of how to survive her brutal assault at age 25. She didn't realize that many other women and men had lived through their own experiences or that, according to the National Crime Victimization Survey, a sexual assault occurs every two minutes in the United States. After her attack, Ream read more about sexual assault and was bothered by the "absence of names and faces" of victims.

"While this absence protects privacy, it also renders us faceless and reinforces a powerful stigma," says Ream. That is why she founded The Voices and Faces Project in 2003.[1] The project shares names, faces, and stories in order to shift the national and international discourse on rape and abuse from blaming victims to holding perpetrators accountable. The Voices and Faces Project web site (www.voicesandfaces.org) features an interactive online "safe zone" with actual survivor stories, a reading room with downloadable literature on rape and abuse, plus links to additional resources. The site had more than 20 million visits and has empowered 300 women to share their personal stories of sexual violence in its first five years of existence.

"At the heart of our work is a simple belief," says Ream, "that public testimony can change the world, making it a more fair, just, and safe place for women. We know that being public is not the right choice for every survivor and we honor those who choose not to do so. But by speaking out, we hope to reverse the attitudes that make it difficult for all survivors to rebuild their lives."

Ream received the 2007–2008 Making a Difference for Women Award presented by Soroptimist International for her work with The Voices and Faces Project. Additionally, she has co-founded Counter Quo (www.counterquo.org) with the Victim Rights Law Center to challenge the way we respond to sexual violence by changing attitudes, culture, and law.

"I enjoyed the benefits of a rewarding career in communications, and I loved doing what I did," Ream continues. "In many ways, I am still calling on those same private sector skills as I work with The Voices and Faces Project. But now instead of raising awareness of a client's product I am raising awareness of a much more urgent and important issue: violence against women and girls. For me, what is exciting is taking my private sector knowledge and experience and applying it to pressing public issues and problems. I know that this has been true for the many people from the private sector who have played a part in building The Voices and Faces Project. When we in the private sector consider ourselves not only professionals, but citizens—with a citizen's obligation to engage in our communities—we can make a real difference."

Most people will never achieve the fame or exposure that lands them in a history book. Leaders, on the other hand, reject the notion that the assurance of recognition is a prerequisite for action. That is the common denominator that Strickland, Montgomery, and Ream share. To do anything less would be to abandon their integrity.

> **The problems that exist in the world today cannot be solved by the level of thinking that created them.**
>
> *—Albert Einstein*

WHY LEADERSHIP IS CRITICAL

Pick a problem . . . any problem. There are plenty to go around: the economy; the environment; global competition; educating our youth; preventing crime, violence, terrorism, illiteracy, teen pregnancy, drug use, shady business dealings, and shady political dealings; saving Social Security; making health care affordable; finding the cure for cancer, heart disease, AIDS, or the common cold; or ensuring your family's financial security.

There is not a single problem that can be solved without leadership because there is no problem that can be solved without people. Even if you had the answer, its implementation requires cooperation and collaboration. And, there are always detractors, naysayers,

> **Without trust there is no cooperation between people, teams, departments, and divisions. Without trust each component will protect its own immediate interests to its long-term detriment and to the detriment of the entire system.**
>
> *—W. Edwards Deming*

those with a stake in the status quo, and people who simply believe that their idea is better.

The old, tired theories of leadership based on the power of position and authoritarian models of persuasion are not compatible with today's need for collaboration, cooperation, and commitment. They will be even less effective as a tool for influencing change and positive action tomorrow.

The most effective leaders will be those who command respect. The absence of trusted leadership creates a vacuum that allows chaos to flourish. Mistrust creates friction that reduces loyalty, communication, productivity, performance, and profits. Compliance can be mandated, but commitment is volunteered to those leaders who earn the trust of others through the integrity of their thought, communication, and action.

A FAILURE TO LEAD

A March 19, 2009 editorial appearing in the *Dallas Morning News* asked an important question: Whatever happened to shame?

The piece was written after executives in the troubled Financial Products division for insurance-industry giant AIG received $165 million (later revised to over $218 million) in bonuses. The outrage was fueled by the company's acceptance of $182.5 billion in government aid to continue its operation. Legally, neither the company nor the executives receiving the bonus money had done anything wrong. In fact, the legal argument had been made that it would be a violation of employment contracts not to pay the bonuses.

The public was outraged. Elected officials from both political parties called the bonuses unconscionable. The president of the United States publicly ridiculed the action.

The *Dallas Morning News* editorial makes an important point:

Shame is the feeling you get when you don't live up to ethical expectations. It's not the same thing as guilt, which is the condition of having done something immoral or criminal. It is possible to behave legally but shamefully.

In a culture that celebrates self-gratification and self-enrichment, is it any wonder that people have lost a sense of what it means to behave disgracefully?

The U.S. military, the one institution in American life where honor is openly embraced, is far and away the most trusted institution in our society, according to opinion polls. That's no coincidence.[2]

The legality of paying and accepting bonuses in spite of the company's poor performance and subsequent government assistance is a correct response to the question of "Who is right?" Feeling a sense of shame and responding with dignity, duty, and respect is the correct response to the question of "What is right?" Action based on who is right is almost always self-serving. Action based on what is right is always a sign of leadership.

TRADITIONAL PRINCIPLES TO THE RESCUE

Stephen Covey discussed the difference between the personality ethic and the character ethic in his classic book *The Seven Habits of Highly Effective People.*

The *personality ethic*, which began to emerge after World War I, suggests that success was a "function of personality, of public image, of attitudes, skills and techniques, that lubricate the process of human interaction."[3] Some aspects of the personality ethic—such as the importance of a positive attitude—are valuable. Other aspects—such as faking interest in others or using techniques to gain others' approval—can be manipulative and deceptive.

The *character ethic* stresses traditional principles such as integrity, honor, courage, duty, loyalty, humility, and fidelity. The character ethic is found in Benjamin Franklin's autobiography; the Golden Rule; and the Scout Oath, Law, and motto. It is built on the realization that who we are—rather than the techniques we use—determines our ultimate success.

The personality ethic celebrates self-gratification, posturing, and positioning. The character ethic promotes doing what's right. The personality ethic is an external solution. The character ethic is an internal solution. Applying an external solution to an internal problem never works. Sure it might make your situation "look" better from the outside. But in the end, the perception that all is well gives way to the reality that substance—not splash—is required to influence others over the long run.

In times of crisis, challenge, and change, the techniques of the personality ethic lose their effectiveness unless they are clearly secondary to the primary principles that define the character ethic. You can look good for a while, but sooner or later, you will be exposed.

However, leading by the traditional principles of integrity, duty, and honor provide no guarantee that you escape the judgment that comes from others disagreeing with your course of action.

WILLIAM S. SESSIONS: A COMMITMENT TO INTEGRITY-DRIVEN LEADERSHIP

William Sessions was raised on the principles of integrity, duty, honor, and accountability. The principles are deeply ingrained in his family's character. His father wrote the first *God and Country* handbook for the Boy Scouts of America. He is an Eagle Scout and recipient of the Distinguished Eagle Scout Award. His son, Pete, and his grandson, Bill, are both Eagle Scouts. And his son is also a recipient of the Distinguished Eagle Scout Award.

William Sessions's career as a public servant includes an appointment as the chief of the Government Operations Section, Criminal Division for the U.S.

Department of Justice; U.S. attorney for the Western District of Texas; United States District Judge; and director of the Federal Bureau of Investigation.

I spoke with Judge Sessions about the process he uses when confronted with a difficult leadership decision. Without hesitation he responded:

> *The first thing on which I rely as a leader is the Scout Oath and Promise. It is a very demanding oath, and I have been able to abide by it because I took seriously the commitment to do my best. It doesn't guarantee that you will be perfect or won't make mistakes. It doesn't guarantee that you won't be harassed or charged. But if you say that you are going to do your best, you will be all right.*

Sessions has made and seen more than his share of difficult leadership situations. The FBI was embroiled in a lawsuit by Hispanic agents alleging discrimination when he took over as director. During his tenure, he faced both the Ruby Ridge and Branch Davidian altercations in 1992 and 1993, respectively.

About the discrimination suit by agents Sessions says, "The decision stung the Bureau, and it angered some agents. But it was right, and we set about correcting it." He continued, "Some decisions you know will be questioned and disagreed with. I try to answer two questions: (1) How will the decision you are making benefit the organization, agency, or the country? and (2) What do you want to have said about the outcome?"

Do not confuse Sessions's second question as a willingness to sacrifice what is right for what looks right. Nothing could be further from the truth. In fact, it was his commitment to doing what is right that contributed to his removal from the role of director of the FBI.

Sessions was accused, dismissed, and ultimately vindicated of any wrongdoing for alleged ethics violations.

Lost in the coverage was a disagreement about the FBI's relationship with the president. Sessions believed that maintaining the Bureau's position as an independent agency would prevent it from becoming a political arm for any president. It is a principle that Sessions applauds his predecessors for maintaining despite occasional battles with other presidents. And it is a principle on which he was willing to stake his job.

I asked Sessions if he ever thought about resigning in the midst of seeing his reputation attacked daily in the media. He responded, "When you are in a difficult situation, you always think about what would ease the pain." So why didn't he resign? Sessions said, "You stand firm for what you believe, and you accept the results of that decision."[4]

SEVEN PRINCIPLES THAT WILL SERVE YOU WELL

We defined integrity in Chapter 2 as completeness, honesty, and transparency in thought, communication, and action. It is the basic ingredient in a leadership approach that is well suited to address the complexities of our problems, lack of trust in our institutions, and need for interconnectedness in our relationships.

Clearly, William Sessions qualifies as do Bill Strickland, John Montgomery, and Anne Ream. The people who accepted bonuses after making business decisions that, arguably, could have bankrupted their company . . . not so much.

If you have ever painted a room in your home with a custom color, you know that the final product begins with a base color. Think of integrity and a bias for action as the base colors from which your custom color is blended. The final product—even though it bears no resemblance to the base—will not be correct unless the blend began with the proper foundation.

It is the same for the leadership required to solve the challenges we experience today and will face tomorrow. As we look ahead, here are seven principles that will serve you well as you create your own customized version of integrity-driven leadership:

1. **Courage:** Every difficult decision requires courage. It doesn't matter if you are starting a new business, challenging the status quo, ending a business or practice that is no longer relevant, or standing up to do what is right. Be bold in your action. Be resolute in your principles, and be honest in your communications.

The courage to follow your dreams (like John Montgomery and Anne Ream) or stand up for your convictions (like William Sessions) is the refusal to give up on what you believe because of fear or doubt.

2. **Service:** We often define service as meeting the needs, wants, and expectations of our customers or constituents. This transactional definition is a worthwhile goal, but what would happen if service turned into a transformational experience? What would be different if we moved from servicing others to serving others—not from a position of weakness but out of a desire to ensure others' highest needs are met? Max DePree, former CEO of the Herman Miller Corporation, said, "The first responsibility of a leader is to define reality. The last is to say thank you. In between, the leader is both a debtor and a servant."[5]

3. **Kindness:** Do you actively look for ways to be kind to others? Do you hold the door for the delivery person with an armful of boxes? Do you hold the elevator for the person running to catch it in your office building . . . even if you are running late? One of the most vivid memories from my interview with H. Ross Perot was that he came out of his office to greet me in the reception area and walked me to the elevator at the end of our time together. His graciousness contributed to my sense of respect. Kindness breeds civility and, in doing so, increases the opportunity for collaboration, earns trust, and opens the door for honest discourse.

4. **Sustainability:** This is a principle that has application in virtually every area of our lives including interpersonal, biological, ecological, economic, and organizational systems. The principle of sustainability requires that we look beyond the immediate decision to anticipate the consequences, intended and unintended. It challenges us to think of the impact of our choices and to practice stewardship of our resources.

5. **Passion:** You are competing for the hearts and minds of those you aspire to lead. And, there are a seemingly infinite number of options from which they can choose. Bill Strickland isn't merely interested in changing lives and communities. He is passionate about it, and it is that passion that attracts others to his mission and cause. The individuals and groups you lead are waiting to be inspired and engaged. They want to feel connected to something important, and they are waiting and watching to see if you fill that role. John Wesley, the eighteenth-century evangelist, noted: "When you set yourself on fire, people love to come and see you burn."

6. **Preparation:** The Scout Oath talks about being mentally awake. The Scout motto is "Be prepared." Both are wise counsel in today's rapidly changing world. William Sessions told me, "Being prepared is the hallmark of a good lawyer. If a lawyer is not competent, it is probably because he is not prepared." The same can be said of leaders in every walk of life. Become a student of your business, industry, and profession. Stay informed. Don't abdicate the information you need to know to make an effective decision. Be on the lookout for changes, threats, and opportunities. To paraphrase Sessions, if a leader is unsuccessful it is probably because he hasn't adequately prepared.

7. **Accountability:** Responsibility is given. It can be accepted or not. Accountability is responsibility accepted freely and without reservation. Most of the challenges that leaders and their organizations face today have identifiable solutions. In our businesses, we know how to tell the truth to customers, treat employees as adults, deliver what we promise, and do things right the first time. In our families, schools, and communities, we know how to teach children right from wrong, combat childhood obesity, or solve any number of problems that frustrate us. We don't need more information, and if we do it is readily available through any

number of resources. The world needs more leaders who demonstrate accountability.

Extraordinary results occur when a leader combines these seven traditional principles with integrity in thought, communication, and action. A reputation for credibility is established; hope and confidence are fostered, and people are influenced to achieve more than they may have thought possible in pursuit of something they embrace as important. That's what it will take to tackle the challenges we face in the future.

A REASON TO BELIEVE

There are those who believe that we have reached and perhaps exceeded the limits of our current institutions and the models on which they were built. They point to the failures in business, education, government, families, and religion as proof that we are ill-equipped to address the challenges that face us today and will, most assuredly, increase tomorrow.

> **One hallmark of an optimistic people is a belief that one individual can make a difference.**
>
> —*James Kouzes and Barry Posner*

I reject that assumption and remain an optimist. Here are five reasons why:

1. **The example of history:** Every generation faces its problems. Every organization has tough times when it is struggling to regain equilibrium, take performance to a higher level, or launch a new idea. History provides us with examples of leaders with integrity and character that rose to the occasion and led what may have seemed like a rebellion but ended up being a transformation.

2. **The power of a compelling cause:** The patriots revered as the founding fathers of the United States were, at the beginning,

ordinary people who decided to stand on principle and take action. They were, in fact, rebels who gave their lives for a purpose in which they believed.

3. **The capacity for achievement:** The imagination of the human mind and the capacity of individuals engaged for a common purpose to achieve amazing things are infinitely renewable resources. The solutions to the challenges we face will surface when leaders prove that they can be trusted to create an environment that encourages and nurtures excellence.

4. **The flight to value and values:** In times of crisis and change, people run toward value and values. Like investors who flee equities for the safety of the bond markets, cash, or precious metals in an economic downturn, followers seek trusted leaders who share their values and add value to the relationship. Integrity is the gold standard for leaders, and followers will seek the confidence and credibility it brings.

5. **The faith in the next generation of leaders:** The next generation of leaders will bring a comfort level with technology that is unprecedented. They have been uniquely equipped since their youth to work collaboratively in groups. Yes, they can be demanding, want an immediate voice in decisions, and expect more attention than past generations. They also have a tendency to place their loyalty in individuals rather than organizations. That is how they were raised. They have the capacity to become the next great generation when the many positive skills and attributes they bring are combined with the traditional values of integrity, honor, duty, and service. Bill Strickland told me that the receptive response to his presentations at Harvard Business School reinforces his belief that individuals can make a difference. He says that the students at Harvard share something in common with

the youth at his training centers—they all hope that they can succeed and make a difference.

I am convinced that traditional principles articulated in the character-based, integrity-driven models of leadership are more than sufficient to build trust in our leaders, allow individuals to make a difference, and influence others to positive action wherever they may find themselves. What about you?

CHAPTER SEVEN

NOT THE END

It is time for us all to stand and cheer for the doer,
the achiever, the one who recognizes the challenge
and does something about it.

—Vincent Lombardi

THE STRUGGLE OF LEADERSHIP

Living and leading with integrity and earning the trust and confidence of others—these are the struggles of leadership in a world ripe with uncertainty, mistrust, and cynicism.

We know the words to say. Every leader and organization uses them in value statements and every form of communication. The leaders at Enron placed the words Respect, Integrity, Community, and Excellence on a huge banner, coffee mugs, and desktop cards in their corporate headquarters.

Pick a failed leader or organization and more times than not you will also see good intentions . . . at least articulated if not always implemented. Who is going to openly say they don't believe in traditional principles such as integrity, honor, duty, and service? And, that's the problem—everyone says the right words.

Here is the secret: Intention isn't action. Saying you want to be an integrity-driven leader without actually doing the hard work to move closer to your ideal is like saying you want to be healthier by simply thinking about exercise and a sensible diet.

This book was written to make a point . . . several of them actually:

- Leadership has little to do with position and everything to do with your ability to influence others. Everyone leads. The only variables are how and in what direction.

- An integrity-driven approach to leadership is critical to your success today, and it will be even more important in the future. Compliance can be mandated. The commitment, cooperation, and collaboration you need to be successful in a connected world with flattened hierarchies and diverse constituencies are volunteered rather than mandated.

- Leaders operate at three levels: personal, interpersonal, and organizational. Individual integrity precedes interpersonal integrity, and both are required to make organizational integrity a way of life.

- You can do this. The consistent stream of bad examples portrayed in the media might lead you, like the client mentioned in Chapter 1, to believe that you can't be a successful leader by being a "Boy Scout." We have introduced you to presidential candidates, corporate CEOs, government officials, founders of small companies, community leaders, and regular people from all walks of life. These individuals are diverse in age, gender, background, belief, and occupation. And yet they all share a common commitment to positive action built on a foundation of integrity, honor, duty, and service. They are all "Good Scouts" who have shown that adherence to traditional principles makes them more effective leaders. It is no guarantee that others will always agree with you or that you won't ever make a mistake. But, these principles have stood the test of time because they work.

ISN'T IT MORE DIFFICULT TO KEEP YOUR INTEGRITY TODAY?

I asked that question a lot as I interviewed leaders for this book. Their responses mentioned the increasing complexity of relationships, marketplace competitiveness, and the challenge of staying current on the broad array of issues facing today's leader. But no one said that leading with integrity is necessarily more difficult.

Jose Niño captured the collective sentiment: "Everyone believes that life is a compromise. At the end of the day, you don't have to compromise. It's a choice."

The ease with which the choice is made has a lot to do with your habits. William Sessions likened it to the athlete running a mile. For her or him, this is an easy task. For the confirmed couch potato, it is incredibly difficult.

MAKING THE MOVE

One of the lasting impressions from my 1990 interview with Mary Kay Ash was her comment that she continually worked to refine and sharpen her skills as a leader. Although Ash was a leadership legend, she still looked for ways to improve. That is what integrity-driven leaders do. It is an obligation to maintain completeness, honesty, and transparency in thought, communication, and action.

We have provided a self-assessment at www.onmyhonorbook.net to help you determine your best course of action to improve your skills. You will also find a planning template to help you chart your progress.

You don't have to use our assessment to get started, however. Chances are that you have an idea of the areas on which you want to work if you have made it this far in the book. We've included an abbreviated version of the planning document at the end of this chapter. To stimulate your thinking, we'll discuss five ideas for continuing on your journey toward integrity-driven leadership.

Start with Yourself

This sounds obvious, right? The truth is that while many people believe things need to change, the number of people that are willing to do the hard work of actually changing themselves is considerably smaller.

The personality ethic discussed in Chapter 6 tells us to look for techniques to manage perceptions. A CEO client summarized that approach when he told me in a fit of frustration, "I don't mind being dictatorial. I just don't want to be perceived that way." The character ethic recognizes that focusing on who you are; what you stand for; and how you become more complete, honest, and transparent in every aspect of your life reduces the need to rely on techniques that are soon seen as contrived. Here are several ideas to help:

> **Decide.** Another hokey suggestion, right? Not really when you consider the difference between what's legal and what's right. Doing what is legal requires compliance with the law. You don't have to even comply completely. You just have to stay within acceptable boundaries. Doing what is right is a much more stringent standard. As William Sessions told me, "The law is codified and set. Integrity has a great deal to do with how interested a person is in doing the right thing." It is difficult to teach adults to act and lead with integrity unless they have decided that they want to learn.

> **Get clear on the principles you hold dear.** President Gerald Ford noted, "In the age-old contest between popularity and principle, only those willing to lose for their convictions are deserving of posterity's approval." So what are the principles for which you

would lose your popularity? In Chapter 3, you were given two exercises to complete: (1) write the eulogy you would want delivered after your death, and (2) write what members of your team should expect from you as a leader. If you haven't completed these or similar exercises, schedule an appointment with yourself right now to do so. If you don't know what you stand for, you will fall for anything.

Develop your personal advisory board. There comes a time when each of us needs a different perspective. You can employ a coach, therapist, or counselor. You can even use a friend, mentor, or colleague. Or your advisory board can be virtual. In Chapter 3, we provided six questions that make up the Ethics Litmus Test. Question 5 asked, "How would the person you most admire handle this situation? What would your hero do?" Listing your heroes or heroines and using their examples is a useful tool when you need a different perspective.

Put good stuff in to get smarter. Charlie "Tremendous" Jones, the legendary motivational speaker and founder of Executive Books, is remembered for saying, "You are the same today as you'll be in five years except for two things, the books you read and the people you meet." I believe there is a third thing—the habits you develop. But, new habits are difficult——if not impossible—without new information and insights.

Best-selling author Larry Winget writes:

The sad fact is, on the average, people spend twenty hours per week watching television and less than two hours per week reading. Fifty-eight percent of Americans won't read a nonfiction book after high school. Forty-two percent of university graduates never read another book at all after college. Only 20 percent will buy or read a book this year.[1]

The fact that you are reading this book puts you in the minority. There are other ways to put the good stuff in your head and heart that will make you smarter. You can read magazines, listen to audio podcasts or audio books while commuting, or attend seminars. The important thing is to do something. Leaders are learners. Tradition is a fine heritage, but a lousy excuse for missing an opportunity to improve.

Evaluate and improve. You can tell the serious golfers from the weekend hackers within 30 minutes of arriving at the driving range. The difference can be captured in hitting balls versus practicing. The hackers hit ball after ball after ball without ever watching its flight, thinking about their swing, or taking steps to improve their shot. The amazing thing is that they are surprised when their shots never go where they want them to on the course. The serious golfer intent on improvement practices on specific shots and techniques, evaluates performance, and takes immediate steps to improve. I see the same thing in my seminars. There are typically three types of attendees in my sessions—learners, vacationers, and prisoners. The prisoners are most often found in the required sessions. The vacationers are there to have a good time and be entertained. The learners are serious about improving their skills. They take an honest evaluation of their performance.

What Happens When You Mess Up?

Public apology for a mistake was the norm when the original edition of this book was published in the early 1990s. Leaders apologized early and often. Those days are gone or at least in hiding.

Del Jones, writing in *USA Today,* notes: "As the world comes to grips with the biggest financial crisis in seven decades, the *mea culpa* machine has ground to a halt. Apologies, encouraged in recent years by the crisis management industry, have dried up."[2]

And yet, the public is looking for someone to take responsibility—to say they messed up. That is why we address this subject again here in addition to the discussion in Chapter 5.

Jones continues: "The absence of apologies has fed widespread outrage. Even CEOs in other industries are upset that they must now negotiate their companies through what appears to be an inevitable recession."

The reason for the silence is liability. An apology can be viewed as an admission of guilt. It is okay for an athlete or entertainer to express regret for his embarrassing actions, but admitting to something like the complete disruption of the financial and credit markets carries a multibillion-dollar price tag. Litigation will certainly be evaluated and charges will most likely be brought against those who knowingly committed fraud.

So what is the answer?

I am not a lawyer. You should consult qualified legal counsel if you find yourself in a situation where your actions could result in legal action—charges filed or lawsuits incurred.

The answer, however, is simple if your goal is to take responsibility, restore the trust that has been lost, and regain credibility with others. Three confessions can help any leader get back on track when integrity and trust have been breached:

1. "I did it. I made a mistake."

2. "I am sorry, and I take responsibility."

3. "Here is what I will do to make it right." or "How can I make it right?" (depending on the situation).

Your lawyer's job is to recommend the best course of action to protect you legally. The leader's job is to decide on and implement the best course of action for all concerned.

Strengthen Interpersonal Relationships

The test to determine leadership effectiveness is simple—are people willing to follow you over the long term? The key component is trust.

We discussed five factors that cause mistrust in Chapter 4: Character, Competence, Consistency, Communication, and Courage. These five factors came from a research project conducted in cooperation with consulting companies Pilat-NAI and IRI Consultants to Management in 2004. One surprising finding was that the way we relate to others through communication and consistency of action is the primary cause of mistrust in our relationships. In fact, communication issues represented the largest overall category of responses in the study.[3]

It is clear that leadership requires a relationship. The following ideas are offered as a good place on which to focus your attention.

Move from Service to Serving

Service, in most areas of our lives, has become a series of managed transactions. In the customer care center environment, the people answering your call are measured and rewarded on a variety of factors that someone has determined are important—accuracy, call handling time, being friendly, and others. That is fine if I am calling with a question about my cell phone service. It is not what I'm looking for in a relationship with a leader who inspires trust, respect, and credibility. And yet, there are times when we all feel that the leaders with whom we interact are more interested in providing a service rather than actually serving. Being a servant requires the leaders to put others' needs first, to be humble, and to invest time building the relationship.

H. Ross Perot explained it this way in our conversation, "The troops always eat first." What Perot was saying is that the leader who serves always puts the needs of the followers before his or her own personal needs even if it means going without.

Practice Win-Win

The win-win concept is, in theory, simple: You get what you want and others get what they want. It is the Scout Oath's commitment—to help other people at all times—in action.

Reality paints a different picture. There are times when goals are not compatible and situations where your win is contingent on someone else's loss. There is also the power of our culture. We learn from an early age that there are winners and losers. It is reinforced through every sort of competition and contest from athletics to academics to popularity to entertainment.

I like winning . . . a lot. And, I have come to understand that a singular focus on winning that requires someone else to lose is not always in my best interest if the goal is a stronger interpersonal relationship. It requires me to constrain my competitive nature, work for the greater good, and most important, keep the long-term relationship in mind. A win-win approach to interpersonal relationships requires three things:

1. **Knowing what is important to you.** Not just what is important now, but what is important over the long-term in the relationship;

2. **Knowing what is important to the other person.** This requires a genuine interest in that individual or group. For me, that can occasionally be a challenge. There are people and groups that I just don't like that much. They tick me off. We don't share the same priorities; or more accurately, they don't share my priorities. And they disagree with the course of action I think is correct. But I have to suck it up and do the hard work if the goal is a long-term relationship built on trust and respect; and

3. **Being willing to stay at it until everyone gets a win.** The typical approach is to compromise. That works if neither party is

giving up something that is important to them. But usually, one or both parties feel as if they had to take something less than they really wanted in order to reach a solution. Staying at it until everyone gets a win takes even more work than just understanding what is important to the other person.

Have you noticed how often the word "work" appears in this section? It is not an accident. The more important the outcome, the more challenging it is to achieve a win-win result. The rewards are worth the effort in terms of the quality of the solution and strengthening the relationship. If that is your goal, then win-win is your strategy.

Listen More

You are still the leader, and the final decisions are still left at your feet. That is no excuse for not listening. H. Ross Perot and Rex Tillerson responded almost identically when I asked them how they approached problems: I ask for input from the people who are closest to the situation. Imagine a relationship where you were rarely allowed to speak and never listened to even when you did. Not very satisfying is it? The days of the supreme commander barking orders without considering any input from others are gone. You aren't that smart, and even if you were, very few people would volunteer to follow you.

Share Why and Show How Rather Than Telling What

Like other ideas shared in this book, this one has a dual benefit. You read about the care Mary Kay Ash took in developing others in Chapter 4. The company's performance speaks for itself. The organizational benefit is that you are giving others the knowledge and skills needed to perform more effectively and take on more responsibility in the future. That is reason enough for many people, but there is an interpersonal relationship benefit that extends far beyond the immediate need to develop talent. Find a veteran Mary Kay consultant who actually met Ash while she was alive. Ask about the impact her caring had as that consultant grew into a leader. And, ask if that influence remains today. The ability to influence others long after we cease to be around is the ultimate sign of great leadership.

Hear and Speak the Truth

Valuing candor and honesty is a common habit in organizations that consistently deliver amazing results. It is a trait that is modeled from leaders and expected from everyone. The truth cuts through excuses. The truth allows energy to be devoted to the important work of performing and improving. And the truth—both speaking and hearing—shows that you respect and care about yourself and others.

We typically avoid the truth. We deny the facts. We distort reality to fit our desired picture, and we delude ourselves into thinking that our way is the only way. If you want a better relationship with your customers, learn to hear the truth and speak it in a way that will ensure they will listen to your message. The same applies if you want a better relationship with your employees, team members, colleagues, spouse, children, or constituents. Remember this: Your credibility to speak the truth will increase exponentially with your willingness to hear the truth and your demonstration that you really care about the best interest of others.

Build Your Organization for Integrity in Products, Services, and Relationships

The size, scope, and nature of your organization don't matter. The challenges of building a culture that is committed to integrity in everything you do is one of the leader's most challenging responsibilities. Working on yourself and your interpersonal relationships is the starting point.

Consider the following as you extend your influence to a group of followers. The language relates to the business world, but the principles apply in every situation:

Don't announce a new "Integrity Program." This may sound contradictory after reading the ideas provided in Chapter 5, but programs historically have a starting and an ending date. Programs are viewed with skepticism and cynicism. We've all seen initiatives come and go with little lasting impact. Explain why integrity is important, and then prove its importance in the way you make decisions, develop, reward, and hold people accountable. Keep the focus on the goal of making integrity a way of life. Programs come and go, but the principles of integrity, honor, duty, and service are constant guides.

Conduct an integrity audit. This is the organizational extension of hearing the truth. You need to know how you are perceived by customers, employees, and suppliers. Look at processes and their alignment to ensure you are doing what you said you would do the way you promised it would be done. Involve everyone. Make it a regular part of your operation. Look for opportunities to expand what you are already doing to determine customer and employee satisfaction. Johnson & Johnson continuously surveys its employees on its success or failure in living the company's credo. You can't improve until you know how well you are performing.

Remember and practice the three "Ps" for managing change—patience, purpose, and persistence. Be patient. Change rarely occurs overnight and usually meets with resistance. If people could change easily and overnight many of us would wake up tomorrow being completely healthy at our desired weight. Stay focused on the purpose—to develop an organization that wins the trust of others. It is easy to be pulled by competing priorities. Be persistent. You will not change your organization's reputation for integrity with a few speeches, an article in the company newsletter, posters on the wall, and a new delivery of coffee mugs inscribed with some pithy saying. Those have their place, but changing a reputation for integrity is an immense undertaking. There are no shortcuts to integrity—things that appear to be shortcuts are only detours that can lead you in the opposite direction.

JAMES CASH PENNEY—AN EXAMPLE OF INTEGRITY

On April 14, 1902, 26-year-old James Cash Penney, Thomas M. Callahan, and William Guy Johnson opened the first Golden Rule Store in Kemmerer, Wyoming. As the store prospered, they set up other Golden Rule Stores. Each was operated as a partnership that enabled those responsible for the store's success to share in the profits.

In 1913, when the Golden Rule Stores were incorporated as the JCPenney Company, James Penney met with all the partners in the Golden Rule to discuss the new company. He wanted to make certain their new organization had the same motivation, spirit, and ethical foundation that had made the company successful. The 36 men at that meeting adopted a company motto built on four words: Honor, Confidence, Service, Cooperation. This motto was later abbreviated to HCSC and used in the company emblem. That meeting also produced the "Penney Idea," seven principles that are reflected in the company's operation to this day. They are:

1. To serve the public, as nearly as we can, to its complete satisfaction.

2. To expect for the service we render a fair remuneration and not all the profit the traffic will bear.

3. To do all in our power to pack the customer's dollar full of value, quality, and satisfaction.

4. To continue to train ourselves and our associates so that the service we give will be more and more intelligently performed.

5. To improve constantly the human factor in our business.

6. To reward men and women in our organization through participation in what the business produces.

7. To test our every policy, method, and act in this wise: "Does it square with what is right and just?"

The JCPenney Company has become an institution in America because of its commitment to honoring these principles. The company has never suffered a serious ethical crisis in its history. W.R. Howell, former chairman of the board, shared this example of Penney's integrity in one of his speeches:

> *Mr. Penney was on the board of directors of a bank in Florida during the Great Depression. He had nothing to do with the day-to-day running of the business, but his name and reputation were instrumental in bringing in depositors. Well, like so many other financial institutions at the time, the bank folded and there was an outcry from depositors. Many could not understand how a bank associated with Mr. Penney could fail while he remained a multimillionaire. Mr. Penney was so anguished by the event that he used a large part of his personal fortune to pay the depositors what they had lost. He clearly was under no legal obligation to do so. He simply felt it was the right thing to do. That's the kind of person he was—and that's the kind of legacy he left. He never forgot that when you're a company that serves the public, what you are and how you conduct yourself become a part of your name and reputation.*[4]

The policies and principles of integrity that Penney first formalized in 1913 with the Penney Idea are reflected today in the company's culture, commitment to social responsibility, and honoring of inclusiveness and diversity. The retail market changes like the seasons, and there are always examples of highfliers that become the flavor of the month for investors. And yet, JCPenney continues to honor the principles articulated by Penney and the company founders—to add value, treat people with respect, and create a workforce that is engaged to deliver great service. How many companies do you know that have a history dating back to 1902? That is an example and history of which any leader can be proud.

Demand Integrity from the Leaders Who Represent You

We get the leaders we deserve. Maybe not in the microsense, but certainly from a macroperspective.

Am I saying that the individuals who saw their retirement savings stripped away in any of the numerous scandals and crashes between 2000 and 2008 responsible for their own demise?

Yes and no. Let's take the real estate and credit collapse of 2008 as an example. Unless you are a corporate board member or large enough investor to have access to information the rest of us don't receive, you didn't have a clue about the poor decisions and, in some cases, outright fraud that was going on in the offending financial institutions and mortgage companies. But others did, and they allowed greed and poor judgment to place an entire economy at risk.

Individuals contributed as well by taking mortgages that they knew they could not afford. They leveraged themselves to the hilt and defaulted on their obligations rather than acting responsibly.

Finally, the elected officials who pushed for expanding home ownership to the point that bad decisions were being made for political purposes share the blame as well.

That means everyone shares some part of the blame either directly or indirectly.

There is no greater example of getting the leaders we deserve than America's long history of dissatisfaction with its elected leaders. And yet, we continue to elect those we do not trust to act in our best interests.

The Gallup organization reported that 18 percent of Americans approved of the job the U.S. Congress was doing for the period of October 3 to October 5, 2008, one month before the general election. Seventy-seven percent disapproved and 5 percent were undecided.[5]

With this much dissatisfaction, you would suspect a substantial, if not wholesale, change in the membership of Congress. The facts tell a different story.

All 435 seats of the U.S. House of Representatives were up for election in 2008. Thirty-three individuals (6 Democrats and 27 Republicans) retired and chose not to run again. That leaves 402 seats with incumbents on the ballot. Four incumbents were defeated in their party's primary elections, and 19 lost their bid for reelection in the general election. Approximately 95 percent of incumbents to the U.S. House of Representatives were reelected.[6]

Numerous explanations have been provided over the years for this phenomenon. The ability of incumbents to raise more money for campaign advertising or to bring projects that infuse money into the local economy doesn't matter, however, unless the majority of voters put them in office. Leaders being held accountable for acting with integrity will make a difference. The only question is our courage to demand it.

Grow Future Generations of Integrity-Driven Leaders

Two statistics jumped out from those offered in Chapter 5:

- 98 percent of students surveyed believed that it is important to be a person of good character.

- 59 percent of the students agreed that successful people do what it takes to win, even if others consider it cheating.

Most of us grew up knowing the difference from right and wrong and the importance of integrity. We consciously avoid violating our values in the important areas of our lives; we don't commit murder, robbery, rape, treason, or any of the "major sins."

The typical challenges we face are the choices between right and also right or between wrong and less wrong. We are confronted with the decision to sell out our integrity in order to achieve something that we desire—a better job, promotion, status, wealth, or even acceptance. The messages promoting a "do whatever it takes" philosophy of life and leadership are increasing. We must actively develop future generations of integrity-driven leaders.

Rex Tillerson told me:

The challenge of instilling these values is more and more difficult. Youth today are bombarded in so many ways and so many different mediums. Youth get portrayals of what business leaders look like and what government leaders look like that are just perverted because so much of it focuses on the exceptions that behave badly. They are convinced that when you get out there in business that it's a dog-eat-dog world and that all is fair in love and war. That's just not the way it is.[7]

Roger Staubach, Hall of Fame professional football player and founder of The Staubach Company, agrees, "Having the ability to take out of life and give back is what I look for in someone I can trust. This is someone who'll say they are sorry when they make a mistake, say thank you when they're appreciative, and have the ability to put themselves in someone else's shoes. They have balance in their life and put others above their own pursuits." Staubach goes on to say, "A leader has responsibilities to be what they say they are."[8]

If you are not helping grow other leaders, you are not really leading. There are several ways you can help.

Support Character-Building Programs and Education

Zig Ziglar, in the Foreword for the first edition of this book, noted: "According to the Thomas Jefferson Research Institute, in the 1770s over 90 percent of our educational thrust was aimed at teaching moral values. At that time, most of the education was handled in the home, church, or church-supported schools. By 1926, the percentage of moral training had reduced to 6 percent, and by 1951 the percentage was so low you could not even measure it."[9]

William Kilpatrick, a contributing author to the book *Why Johnny Can't Tell Right from Wrong*, suggests that the decline in teaching traditional principles might be traced to an assumption that our youth inherently believe in honesty, integrity, duty, and honor. Based on that assumption, educators use dilemmas or problems to generate conversation. The result is that students can come to believe that there are few absolutes when it comes to principles. Kilpatrick writes, "The danger in focusing on problematic dilemmas such as these is that a student may begin to think that all of morality is similarly problematic. After being faced with quandary after quandary of the type that would stump Middle East negotiators, students will conclude that right and wrong are anybody's guess."[10]

The alternative is to actively support character-building programs that teach traditional principles and how to apply them. There are often competing choices, to be sure. But, we are better equipped to make those choices when a foundation has been laid that teaches principles and their application. Growing future generations of integrity-driven leaders is important. Give your time and financial support to programs such as the Boy Scouts and Girl Scouts. Enroll the children and teens you influence. Sponsor a local Scouting troop. Encourage the community leaders where you live to actively support Scouting. Support other faith- and community-based character-building programs in your community. Encourage schools in your area to teach character rather than simply discussing values. The principles that form the foundation of integrity-driven leadership are not transmitted through time and space. They are taught, and the earlier you can begin, the better the result.

NOTEWORTHY BOYS SCOUTS AND GIRL SCOUTS

Today, there are 28 million Scouts—youth and adults, boys and girls, in 160 countries around the world. In the United States, more than 112 million youth have been taught the lessons of honor, duty, integrity, and service through the Boy Scouts of America since 1910.[11] More than 50 million girls have learned about character in the Girl Scouts of America since 1912.[12]

The alumni of these character-building organizations include leaders in every field of endeavor. Many of them are recognizable names. Others are equally accomplished though less familiar. Many of these distinguished individuals have been profiled and interviewed in this book. Here is a sample of the other individuals who have benefited from the Boy Scouts and Girl Scouts programs:

Henry Aaron	United States	Baseball player, home run king
Madeline Albright	United States	Former Secretary of State
Neil Armstrong	United States	Astronaut, first man on moon, from Wapakoneta, OH
Sir Richard Attenborough	United Kingdom	Actor/Director
Willie Banks	United States	Olympic & World record holding track star
William Bennett	United States	Secretary of Education
H.M. Adulyadej Bhumibol	Thailand	King of Thailand

Bikram Shah De Birenda Bir	Nepal	Former King
Michael Bloomberg	United States	Mayor of New York City, founder Bloomberg News
Bill Bradley	United States	Professional basketball star and Senator (NJ)
Sir Richard Branson	United Kingdom	Businessman/ Entrepreneur
Stephen Breyer	United States	Supreme Court Justice
Laura Bush	United States	Former First Lady
Juan Carlos	Spain	King
Linda Chavez-Thompson	United States	Executive Vice President, AFL-CIO
Jacques Chirac	France	Former President
Jean Chrétien	Canada	Former Prime Minister
Hillary Rodham Clinton	United States	Secretary of State, Former Senator, Former First Lady
Lt. Col. Eileen Collins	United States	First female commander of the Space Shuttle
Tsatsos Constantine	Greece	Former President
Sheryl Crow	United States	Singer/Songwriter
Patricia Diaz Dennis	United States	Vice President of Government Affairs, Sprint
William Devries	United States	MD, transplanted first artificial heart

Jean-Louis Dumas-Hermès	France	Chairman of Hermès (fashion design firm)
Gerald Ford	United States	Former President (first Eagle Scout to be president)
Robert M. Gates	United States	Director of CIA and Secretary of Defense
Boutros Ghali	Egypt	Former UN Secretary General
Carl XVI Gustaf	Sweden	King
Kay Bailey Hutchison	United States	Senator
Masaru Ibuka	Japan	Founder of Sony
Elaine Jones	United States	Head of NAACP Legal Defense & Education Fund
J. Willard Marriott, Jr.	United States	President, Marriott Corp.
Sir Paul McCartney	United Kingdom	Musician
Barbara Mikulski	United States	Senator
Sandra Day O'Connor	United States	Associate Justice, Supreme Court
Claire Shipman	United States	White House correspondent for NBC News
Cornelio Sommaruga	Switzerland	Former President of ICRC
Sam Walton	United States	Founder Wal-Mart

| Togo West | United States | Secretary of the Army and Secretary of Veterans Affairs |
| Mohammed bin Zayed | Saudi Arabia | Prince |

To locate your nearest Boy Scout Council, visit www.scouting.org /media/lcl.aspx. To locate your nearest Girl Scout Council, visit www.girlscouts .org/councilfinder/. To learn more about the World Organization of the Scout Movement, visit www.scout.org.

Tell Your Stories and Create Legends

The leaders with whom I spoke while working on this book freely shared their ideas, and more important, they told me their stories and legends. H. Ross Perot spoke of the lessons learned while riding horseback with his father every afternoon after school and shared the practical advice about living and leading from his mother and grandmother. Jose Niño told me about the example set by his father as he labored the fields as a migrant worker. Judi Phares's brief conversation with Peace Corp Director Jack Vaughn while a volunteer in the Truk Lagoon of Micronesia influenced her approach today. William Sessions spoke of the lessons of self-reliance learned as a Boy Scout in Troop 137, in Kearney, Nebraska.

Jane Jacobs wrote, "cultures live through word of mouth and example."[13] They die when people forget. The stories you tell and legends you create—like my father stopping at the stop sign in the middle of nowhere (in Chapter 2)—become etched in the hearts and minds of future generations. They serve as timeless reminders of what is important.

LESSONS I LEARNED WHILE WRITING THIS BOOK

My original idea for this book was to sound a clear clarion call for a return to traditional values. So what has been learned since Marc Bockmon and I published our original work on this subject in 1992?

There is a never-ending supply of bad examples. They continue to stretch the boundaries of fraud, deceit, dishonesty, and corruption. The technology and globalization that offers immense promise also enables those who operate without integrity to perpetrate even larger amounts of mayhem on the world. Additionally, popular culture reinforces behavior that demeans and victimizes rather than empowers and encourages.

There is still an abundance of leaders and organizations that are successful by practicing an integrity-driven approach to leadership. The stories and examples used here are merely a core sample rather than an exhaustive list. You rarely read about these individuals or organizations. The market for good news stories is fairly limited in a 24/7/365 world with news cycles that must continually be fed.

One person really can make a difference. You may not change *the* world, but you can change *your* world. Talk about and support integrity-driven leaders and organizations. Mentor emerging leaders. Set an example by practicing personal and interpersonal integrity. Work to build integrity-driven organizations on your job and in your community.

You can change later in life, but it is more difficult. Values and principles learned in our youth typically stay with us unless we see an important reason to change. So what is your reason to improve as an integrity-driven leader? How will it help you, your relationships, or your effectiveness? If the answer to these questions convinces you that the result is worth the effort, the ideas and strategies in this book will help you.

You never arrive. There is always more to learn. Integrity-driven leadership truly is a journey. Readers of the first edition co-authored with Marc Bockmon know that this edition is very different. Hopefully, my insights have grown over the years. I have come to appreciate the personal struggle that accompanies a decision to be an integrity-driven leader. And, I have seen how living the traditional principles discussed here can transform organizations.

You can behave with honor and integrity and be successful. The evidence from the highest echelons in businesses and government suggest that behaving like a "Good Scout" is one of the best ways to become successful in today's world, and it will be even more important in the future.

It's difficult to know if this book has done its job. Sales is one indicator, and while we hope many people purchase this book, sales provides no evaluation of how many readers put the principles into practice. We could look for the time when leaders and organizations of all types operate daily from a foundation of integrity. That's a noble goal, but we're not sure how to measure it. And, it is presumptuous to believe a single book will have that type of impact.

Maybe the best way to know that this book has done its job is if when someone calls a person of integrity a real "Boy Scout" or "Girl Scout" they mean it for what it is: a sincere compliment and a sign of respect and admiration. In his book, *Presidential Anecdotes,* Paul F. Boller states that President Gerald R. Ford, "was 'Mr. Nice Guy.' He was, someone said, a 'Boy Scout in the White House.'" Boller added, "Even Congressman Paul McCloskey of California, who opposed Ford on vital issues, thought well of him. 'I get tears in my eyes,' he said, 'when I think about Jerry Ford. We love him.'"[14]

That's the kind of reaction you'll get when you operate like a "real Boy Scout" and live and lead with integrity.

There will always be detractors—those who diminish honor; integrity; and the traditional principles that built our great country, our great companies, and our great organizations. They will say that these principles are out of touch today and cannot work tomorrow. But I wouldn't want to be led by them—would you?

THE INTEGRITY-DRIVEN® LEADER ASSESSMENT PROFILE

Integrity-Driven leaders and organizations demonstrate characteristics or patterns of behavior that enable them to earn the trust and confidence of others.

The Integrity-Driven Leader Assessment Profile is a self-assessment tool designed to help you determine how frequently and how effectively you demonstrate these patterns of behavior. It is based on the concepts from the book *On My Honor, I Will: The Blueprint for Integrity-Driven Leadership.*

This instrument will help you identify the strengths on which you want to build and the areas where you have an opportunity to improve. And, it will help you become a leader who consistently influences others to deliver results through the power of integrity.

Use this tool to benchmark your current level of competency, and then refer to it regularly to evaluate your growth and development. This will allow you to focus your efforts and grow more quickly into the leader you want to be.

Instructions: Please follow these steps carefully to complete and score the profile.

1. **Complete the profile.** Read each of the 25 statements, and circle the number on the rating scale that most accurately describes your performance for each statement.

2. **Score the profile.** Transfer your ratings for each statement to the tally box on the last page of the instrument. Add the scores for each competency or

behavior and divide the total by the number shown following the slash (/) to determine the percentage total for each area.

Example: A score of 0.25 in the Tally Box represents by 25% on the Assessment Profile Graph.

3. **Create your assessment profile graph.** Use the total score for each competency to draw a horizontal bar graph on the grid provided.

4. **Develop your plan.** Use the results of your assessment profile to create your own professional development plan. You may want to share your results with your manager or a peer you trust to confirm and clarify your results.

5. **Act on the results.** Review your plan regularly. Make a conscious effort to maximize one strength and improve one area where improvement is needed for thirty days and then reevaluate your performance. Keep a journal or notes to record your progress. When you have made the progress you desire in a specific area, choose another area on which to work.

Remember: The accuracy of this assessment is in direct proportion to the honesty of your responses.

INTEGRITY-DRIVEN® LEADER ASSESSMENT PROFILE

The following statements are designed to help you identify patterns of behavior and performance that affect your success as a leader. Read each of the 50 statements carefully then circle the number from 1 to 5 that most closely describes the extent to which your leadership performance and behavior matches the statement.

1	2	3	4	5
Never display this behavior or performance	Rarely display this behavior or performance	Display this behavior or performance about half of the time	Almost always display this behavior or performance	Always display this behavior or performance

		1	2	3	4	5
1.	I have complete clarity on my values, beliefs, and priorities. I have identified what is important in every area of my life. I know what I stand for and what I stand against.					
2.	I am loyal to my values and beliefs. The things that are important to me do not change on a whim or without careful evaluation. I hold on to my principles, beliefs, and values without being rigid.					
3.	I am consistent. Others can depend on me to act or react in similar ways in similar situations.					
4.	My actions match my principles and my words. What I believe on the inside is reflected in how I act, behave, and perform on the outside.					
5.	I demonstrate commitment to the people, principles, and priories that I hold as important. I am an active participant rather than an innocent bystander in living my life with integrity.					
6.	I base my decisions on the standard of what is right rather than what is convenient. I do the right thing even when it is unpleasant or inconvenient. I stand up for what's right. I have the courage of my convictions.					
7.	I look out for and demonstrate concern for others. I consider the greater good in my decisions. I help others and operate from the basis of "what is right" rather than "who is right."					
8.	My relationships with others—especially those with whom I am close—are authentic and transparent. I don't pretend to be something that I am not or seek to hide the real me.					

	1	2	3	4	5
9. I actively listen to what others have to say. I seek to understand and not prejudge different and opposing perspectives on issues.					
10. I actively build and foster relationships built on trust rather than relying on fear or utility to exert power over others.					
11. I consciously attempt to help others succeed. I act in others best interest even when it has no immediate payoff for me personally.					
12. I can and do speak freely and honestly— without being rude or condescending—to others. Others can count on me to speak the truth					
13. I actively work toward win-win outcomes when faced with conflict. Others do not have to lose in order for me to feel that I have won.					
14. I openly share information with others whenever possible. I do not withhold information from others that they need to be successful. I do not "spin" information for my personal gain.					
15. I invest the time and effort to build and maintain relationships with individuals and groups that are important to me.					
16. My organization has a reputation for honesty, value, and integrity.					
17. My organization's leaders set a good example of integrity.					
18. People at all levels of my organization clearly understand what is expected of them in areas of productivity, quality, service, job performance, and integrity.					

	1	2	3	4	5
19. Everyone in my organization is united behind the common goals of providing quality products and services to customers in a manner that communicates honesty, value, and integrity.					
20. Decisions are made based on what's right for all parties and not on the basis of tradition or political positioning.					
21. Leaders and managers are held accountable for the development of people.					
22. Individuals are rewarded for their performance that demonstrates integrity.					
23. My organization deals swiftly with individual performance that violates the trust of others.					
24. Individuals are continually encouraged to upgrade their technical and relationship-building skills.					
25. The organization acts responsibly toward the welfare of the community as a whole.					

TALLY BOX
Competency Score

1. Master the discipline of personal integrity	1___ 2___ 3___ 4___ 5___ 6___ 7___	Total _____/35 =	_____
2. Master the art of interpersonal integrity	8___ 9___ 10___ 11___ 12___ 13___ 14___ 15___	Total _____/40 =	_____
3. Master complexities of organizational integrity	16___ 17___ 18___ 19___ 20___ 21___ 22___ 23___ 24___ 25___	Total _____/50 =	_____

RESULTS RULE! LEADER ASSESSMENT PROFILE GRAPH

	20%	25%	50%	75%	100%
1. Master the discipline of personal integrity	➜				
2. Master the art of interpersonal integrity	➜				
3. Master the complexities of organizational integrity	➜				

Name: _____ Date: _____

Target date for review: _____

PROFESSIONAL DEVELOPMENT GOALS:

Strengths on Which to Build	Opportunities for Improvement
1.	1.
2.	2.
3.	3.
4.	4.

NOTES

CHAPTER ONE

1. James Patterson and Peter Kim, *The Second American Revolution* (New York: William Morrow, 1994), 26.

2. "Reuters/DecisionQuest Poll Shows Most Americans Have Lost Trust in Leaders over the Last Four Years," September 29, 2004, http://www.decisionquest.com/press_center.php?NewsID=97.

3. "U.S. Public Widely Distrusts Its Leaders," May 23, 2006, http://www.zogby.com/templates/printnews.cfm?id=1116.

4. "Trust in Political Leaders Slipping: Poll," May 30, 2005, http://www.cbc.ca/canada/story/2005/05/30/poll-canadians050530.html.

5. Susan Hattis Rolef, "Public Trust in Parliament—A Comparative Study," The Knesset Information Division, May 9, 2006, http://www.knesset.gov.il/mmm/data/pdf/me01417.pdf.

6. Thomas L. Friedman, *The World Is Flat: A Brief History of the Twenty-First Century* (New York: Farrar, Straus, Reese, and Giroux, 2005), 421.

7. "Gallup Study Indicates Actively Disengaged Workers Cost U.S. Hundreds of Billions Each Year," March 19, 2001, http://www.mobilityagenda.org/gallup.pdf. Subsequent studies have confirmed that disengagement is a challenge in countries and industries throughout the world. See http://www.gallup.com for detailed information.

8. Benjamin Franklin, *The Autobiography of Benjamin Franklin* (New York: Macmillan, 1962).

9. Sam Walton with John Huey, *Sam Walton: Made in America* (New York: Bantam Books, 1992), 314–317.

10. All Scouting organizations share a commitment to honor, duty, and service to others. The Scout Oath and Law of the Boy Scouts of America are used in this book. The Scout Oath used in other countries may be slightly different. All members of the World Organization of the Scout Movement, however, share a similar Oath and Law. The World Association of Girl Guides and Girl Scouts promotes similar principles in its programs as do the Baden-Powell Scouts and other members of the World Federation of Independent Scouts.

11. Matthew Kirdahy, "Teaching Leadership, Scout's Honor," *Forbes,* September 4, 2007.

CHAPTER TWO

1. Paul Gewirtz, "On 'I Know It When I See It,'" *Yale Law Journal,* 105 (1996): 1023–1047.

2. Chris Ward, "Five Minutes with Willie Nelson," *Performing Songwriter,* 108 (March–April 2008): 50–51.

3. Henry Givray, personal interview by Randy Pennington, May 2009.

4. James MacGregor Burns, *Leadership* (New York: Harper Torchbooks, 1978), 2–3.

5. Ibid., 427.

6. Ibid., 426.

CHAPTER THREE

1. Gordon Allport, preface to *Man's Search for Meaning,* by Viktor E. Frankl (New York: Washington Square Press, 1984), 12.

2. Victor E. Frankl, *Man's Search for Meaning* (New York, Washington Square Press, 1984), 90.

3. Ibid., 100.

4. Sidney B. Simon, *In Search of Values: 31 Strategies for Finding Out What Really Matters Most to You* (Clayton VIC: Warner Books, 1993).

5. Maggie, McComas, "Atop The Fortune 500: A Survey of the CEOs," *Fortune*, April 28, 1986.

6. "Religion in the Workplace," *Business Week*, November 1, 1999.

7. Tony Campolo, "Staying Balanced in an Unbalanced World," http://www.tonycampolo.org/sermons.php.

8. Kenneth Goodpaster, foreword to *The Winds of Turbulence: A CEO's Reflections on Surviving and Thriving on the Cutting Edge of Corporate Crisis*, by Howard Putnam with Gene Busnar (Canton, OH: Harper Business, 1991).

9. Howard Putnam with Gene Busnar, *The Winds of Turbulence: A CEO's Reflections on Surviving and Thriving on the Cutting Edge of Corporate Crisis* (Canton, OH: Harper Business, 1991), 174–175.

10. Harry Emerson Fosdick, "Six Ways to Tell Right from Wrong," (sermon, Riverside Church, New York, NY, October 30, 1932).

11. "Retarded Boy's 16th Birthday Meal a Lifesaver" *Albany (NY) Times Union*, July 18, 1990, http://www.highbeam.com/doc/1G1-156149379.html (accessed June 19, 2009).

12. "'Gerber Boy' Dead at Age 20" *Post-Tribune (IN)*, February 5, 1995, http://www.highbeam.com/doc/1N1-1084E583C0844CB8.html (accessed June 19, 2009).

13. "Business Notes Goodwill-Time" *Time*, April 16, 1990, http://www.highbeam.com/doc/1S1-1120110096982300.html (accessed June 19, 2009).

14. Rick Hampson, "Disabled Man's Death Is as Hard as His Life: The 'Gerber Boy' Wasn't Supposed to Live a Year; Special Food and Lots of Love Helped Him Reach 20" *Albany (NY) Times Union*, January 27, 1995, http://www.highbeam.com/doc/1G1-156872980.html (accessed June 19, 2009).

15. See note 12.

16. See note 14.

17. See note 2, 98.

18. Proverbs 17:22.

CHAPTER FOUR

1. Blaine Lee, *The Power Principle: Influence with Honor* (New York: Simon & Schuster, 1997), 168.

2. Adapted from Blaine Lee's *The Power Principle: Influence with Honor* (New York: Simon & Schuster, 1997), 168–170. Lee cited the work of Eknath Easwaran's *Gandhi the Man* (Peluma, CA: Nilgiri Press, 1978), from which his work was adapted.

3. "Admiration," *The American Heritage Dictionary of the English Language, Fourth Edition.* Houghton Mifflin, 2004. http://dictionary.reference.com /browse/admiration (accessed October 25, 2008).

4. Stephen R. Covey, *Principle-Centered Leadership* (Orangeville, Ontario: Summit Books, 1991), 108.

5. Ibid, 30.

6. Robert B. Cialdini, *Influence: How and Why People Agree to Things* (New York: William Morrow, 1984), 29.

7. Robert L. Dilenschneider, *A Briefing for Leaders: Communication as the Ultimate Exercise of Power* (New York: Harper Business, 1992), xiii.

8. "Trust," *The American Heritage Dictionary of the English Language, Fourth Edition.* Houghton Mifflin, 2004. http://dictionary.reference.com/browse /trust (accessed October 26, 2008).

9. James Patterson and Peter Kim, *The Day America Told the Truth* (Upper Saddle River, NJ: Prentice Hall Press, 1991), 142–143.

10. *Insights on Leadership,* edited by Larry C. Spears (New York: John Wiley & Sons, 1998), 17.

11. Carl Sewell, personal interview by Randy Pennington, June 2009.

12. Trust Factors @ Work Study completed by Pennington Performance Group and Pilat-NAI. Randy Pennington principal researcher with support from Clinton Wingrove of Pilat-NAI. An executive summary of the research results can be found at www.resultsrule.com.

13. Mary Kay Ash, personal interview by Randy Pennington, August 1990.

CHAPTER FIVE

1. "National Business Ethics Survey," Ethics Resource Center, Arlington VA, 2007.

2. "Report to the President," U.S. Department of Justice, Corporate Fraud Task Force, April 2, 2008, iii.

3. Geoff Colvin, "Business Is Back," *Fortune,* May 14, 2007.

4. "Tarnished Employment Brands Affect Recruiting," *HR Magazine,* November 2004.

5. "Corporate Ethics Affect Employee Productivity," HR Magazine, July 2007.

6. "Report Card on the Ethics of American Youth," Josephson Institute, Los Angeles, CA, 2008, http://charactercounts.org/pdf/reportcard/2008/Q_all.pdf.

7. PollingReport.com, "USA Today/Gallup Poll," January 10–13, 2008, http://www.pollingreport.com/institut.htm.

8. PollingReport.com, "Gallup Poll," June 9–12, 2008, http://www.pollingreport.com/institut.htm.

9. PollingReport.com, "Gallup Poll," December 4–7, 2008, http://www.pollingreport.com/religion.htm.

10. Elizabeth Langton, "Garland Girl Wins Hannah Montana Tickets, Trip with False Essay," *Dallas Morning News,* January 4, 2008.

11. Paul Simon, "The Boy in the Bubble," *Graceland,* compact disc, Rhino/Warner Brothers, 1986.

12. United Press International, "Beech-Nut Settles Out of Court Will Pay $7.5M; Admits No Guilt, *Albany (NY) Times Union,* May 9, 1987.

13. Paula Kurtzweil, "Fake Food Fight," *U. S. Food and Drug Administration FDA Consumer,* March–April 1999, http://vm.cfsan.fda.gov/%7Edms /fdfake.html.

14. Jim Wagner, "Food Fraud," *Food Processing,* January 1, 1993, http://www .allbusiness.com/accounting-reporting/fraud/352548-1.html (accessed June 30, 2009).

15. Bob Jenson, "History of Fraud in America," http://www.trinity.edu /rjensen/415wp/AmericanHistoryOfFraud.htm (accessed June 30, 2009).

16. "Drug Maker to Pay $430 Million in Fines, Civil Damages. (Warner-Lambert Co.)," *FDA Consumer,* July 1, 2004, http://www.highbeam.com /doc/1G1-119510191.html (accessed June 19, 2009).

17. "Bolar Settles Lawsuit. (Bolar Pharmaceutical Company Inc.)," *Chain Drug Review,* February 24, 1992, http://www.highbeam.com/doc /1G1-12073391.html (accessed June 19, 2009).

18. See note 3, 42.

19. See note 3.

20. See note 9.

21. Gary K. Clabaugh and Edward G. Rozycki, "Cheating Trends," in *Preventing Cheating and Plagiarism,* 2nd edition (Oreland, PA: NewFoundations Press, 2003).

22. Ralph Keyes, *The Post-Truth Era: Dishonesty and Deception in Contemporary Life* (New York: St. Martin's Press, 2004), 9.

23. Ibid., 16.

24. See note 6.

25. Robert Lipsyte, "'Jock Culture' Permeates Life," *USA Today,* April 10, 2008.

26. Carol J. Loomis, "Tough Questions for Citigroup's CEO," *Fortune*, November 29, 2004, 118.

27. Susan Pulliam, "Ordered to Commit Fraud, a Staffer, Balked, Then Caved," *Wall Street Journal*, June 23, 2003, 1.

28. "Jayson Blair," http://en.wikipedia.org/w/index.php?title=Jayson_Blair&oldid =295208730 (accessed June 8, 2009).

29. Rick Gosselin, "NFL Draft Preview: Offensive Linemen," *Dallas Morning News*, April 16, 2008.

30. Bob Corbett, *The Cheater's Handbook: The Naughty Student's Bible* (New York: Harper, 1998).

31. See note 22, 5.

32. Watson Wyatt, "WorkUSA—Weathering the Storm: A Study of Employee Attitudes and Opinions," research report, September 2002, http://www .watsonwyatt.com/research/resrender.asp?id=W-557&page=1.

33. Humphrey Taylor, "Why Some Companies Are Trusted and Others Are Not," *The Harris Poll* #28, June 20, 2001, http://www.harrisinteractive .com/harris_poll/index.asp?PID=237.

34. Rex Tillerson, personal interview by Randy Pennington, July 2008.

35. Judi Phares, personal interview by Randy Pennington, December 2008.

36. RTI/Community Management Associates, Inc., "CMA Values," https:// www.cmamanagement.com/webtemplate.asp?id=174.

37. See note 27.

38. Darren Dahl, "Do the Right Thing—or Else," *Inc. Magazine*, November 2004, 48.

39. United States Sentencing Commission. *Federal Sentencing Guidelines Manual, 1992 edition*, (St. Paul, MN: West), 352.

40. "Timing Is Everything: The Optimal Time to Learn from Crises," *Entrepreneur,* Fall 2000, https://www.entrepreneur.com/tradejournals /article/print/73183465.html.

41. Johnson & Johnson, "Credo," http://www.jnj.com/wps/wcm/connect /30e290804ae70eb4bc4afc0f0a50cff8/our-credo.pdf?MOD=AJPERES (accessed June 30, 2009).

42. "1982 Chicago Tylenol Murders," http://en.wikipedia.org/wiki/Tylenol _scare (accessed July 7, 2009).

43. Jim Szaller, "One Lawyer's 25 Year Journey: The Dalkon Shield Saga," *Ohio Trial,* Winter 1999, http://lawandhelp.com/oatl.htm (accessed July 7, 2009).

44. "The Dalkon Shield Story: A Company Rewarded for Its Faulty Product— A.H. Robins Company Inc. Lawsuit." *Healthfacts,* May 1996, http://find-articles.com/p/articles/mi_m0815/is_n204_v21/ai_18349380/ (accessed July 7, 2009).

45. Roberta Bloss, Joseph Corneli, Chris Moon, and Lucas Tomsich, "The Dalkon Shield," *History of Science* 3333 H, December 8, 1997, http:// www1.umn.edu/scitech/dalkfina.htm.

46. J. Madeleine Nash and Michael S. Serrill, "A Panel Tries to Judge a Judge," *Time,* July 23, 1984, http://www.time.com/time/magazine /article/0,9171,952466,00.html.

47. Kenneth Labich, "The New Crisis in Business Ethics," *Fortune,* April 20, 1992, 167.

48. Ibid, 168.

CHAPTER SIX

1. For information on The Voices and Faces Project, visit www.voicesandfaces .org.

2. Editorial "Whatever Happened to Shame?" *Dallas Morning News*, March 19, 2009. Documents released the week of March 16–20, 2009, showed that 73 AIG employees received bonuses of more than $1 million and five received bonuses of more than $4 million. The bonuses were awarded as retention pay through agreements established prior to the receipt of Federal funds in 2008 to continue the company's operation and prior to the appointment of Mr. Liddy as CEO.

3. Stephen R. Covey, *The Seven Habits of Highly Effective People* (New York: Simon & Schuster, 1989).

4. The Honorable William Sessions, personal interview by Randy Pennington, April 2008.

5. Max DePree, *Leadership Is an Art* (New York: Doubleday, 1989), 9.

CHAPTER SEVEN

1. Larry Winget, *People are Idiots and I Can Prove It* (New York: Gotham Books, 2009), 134.

2. Del Jones, "Why 'Sorry' Isn't in Many CEO's Vocabularies Anymore," *USA Today*, October 21, 2008.

3. You can download the study's Executive Summary at http://www resultsrule.com/trust_factors_survey.htm.

4. This speech was given in October 1990. The text was provided by the JCPenney company for inclusion in the original edition of this book.

5. This number fluctuates with every poll, but Congress's disapproval ratings never dipped below 50 percent and went as high as 77 percent between September 12, 2005 and March 8, 2009. PollingReport.com is a nonpartisan resource on trends in American public opinion. The site contains information from a number of resources. The findings reported here were found at www.pollingreport.com/CongJob.htm.

6. Election results analyzed from information contained at http://en.wikipedia
   .org/wiki/United_States_House_of_Representatives_elections,_2008.

7. Rex Tillerson, personal interview by Randy Pennington, June 2008.

8. K. Shelby Skrhak, "Captain America," *Success,* July 2009, 72.

9. Zig Ziglar, foreword to *On My Honor, I Will: How One Simple Oath Can
   Lead You to Success in Business,* by Marc Bockmon and Randy Pennington
   (New York: Warner, 1992).

10. Kilpatrick, William. "How Not to Teach Morality." Chapter 4 in *Why
    Johnny Can't Tell Right from Wrong and What We Can Do About It,* edited
    by J. H. Clarke (New York: A Touchstone Book, 1992): 78–95. Available
    online through the Catholic Education Resource Center, http://catholice-
    ducation.org/articles/education/ed0087.html.

11. Boy Scouts of America, "BSA at a Glance," www.scouting.org/Media
    /FactSheets/02-501.aspx (accessed June 10, 2009).

12. Girl Scouts of the USA, "Who We Are: Facts," www.girlscouts.org/who
    _we_are/facts (accessed June 10, 2009).

13. Jane Jacobs, *Dark Age Ahead* (New York: Random House, 2004), 5.

14. Paul F. Boller, *Presidential Anecdotes* (New York: Penguin Books, 1981).

ABOUT THE AUTHOR

———— ✳ ————

R ANDY PENNINGTON IS A resource to leaders who expect results. He is a 20-plus-year business performance veteran, award-winning author, and consultant who has worked with and presented to many of this country's best-known organizations including Alabama Power Company, Motorola, LaSalle Bank, SmithBucklin, Hyatt Hotels and Resorts, Texas A&M University, Exxon, Sprint, Huntsman Chemical, and State Farm Insurance, in addition to government agencies at the local, state, and national level. Additionally, he serves as an adjunct instructor in the Cox Business Leadership Center at Southern Methodist University.

Randy's background is a unique blend of line, staff, and consulting experiences ranging from frontline employee to senior executive. His personal work experience has taken him from a locker room attendant at a municipal swimming pool to consulting in the boardrooms of corporate America and presenting to audiences throughout the world. Along the way, he's been a

- senior executive in a start-up mental health facility,

- recreation therapist in a psychiatric hospital,

- CFO of a multimillion-dollar professional services firm,

- tire and appliance salesman,

- Chairman of the Board for a $17 million nonprofit and multimillion-dollar foundation,

171

- entrepreneur, and

- professional musician at Six Flags Over Texas.

Randy's ideas and comments have appeared in the *New York Times,*
Entrepreneur, Leadership Excellence, on CNN, Fox News, and the ABC radio network. His book, *Results Rule!,* received the 2007 Best Books Award
from USA Book News. Randy has been inducted into the National Speakers Association CPAE Speaker Hall of Fame, and he lives in Addison,
Texas, with his wife Mary and their three dogs.

For information regarding presentations, seminars, leadership retreats,
and consulting service, please contact:

Pennington Performance Group
4004 Winter Park Lane
Addison, Texas 75001
972.980.9857 or 800.779.5295 (U.S.)
www.penningtongroup.com
www.resultsrule.com

ACKNOWLEDGMENTS

——————— ✳ ———————

E VERY EFFORT TO EXPAND knowledge, encourage thinking, and inspire action is a shared process. This one is no different. *Thank You* to ...

- The leaders who participated in this book: Your willingness to share your stories makes the journey to integrity-driven leadership come alive.

- Nancy Marcus Land: You pushed me to be a better writer: Your insight, counsel, and editing prowess were more valuable than you know.

- Matthew Land and the PDC team: You guys are so good to work with. The book looks great, and you were very patient.

- Robert Lee Edmonds and David C. Scott at PenlandScott: You challenged me to re-think my conceptual understanding of what it takes to be an integrity-driven leader.

- My buddies in the American Speakers Society (A.S.S.): You are great friends, incredible talents, and that is all I am allowed to say.

- My other friends and colleagues in the business: There are too many of you to list, but you know who you are. Thanks for your support.

- Marc Bockmon, the co-author of my first effort on this subject: You are missed.

- Charlie Brown: My Eagle Scout friend through thick and thin. We've seen and shared it all. And, we learned what integrity means along the way.

- Spencer, Katie, and Jackson: Three of the best friends ever who just happen to be great dogs.

- And to my wife, Mary: You are the best, and I can't imagine taking this ride with anyone else but you.

INDEX